THE WOUNDS WITHIN

THE WOUNDS WITHIN

A VETERAN, A PTSD THERAPIST, AND A NATION UNPREPARED

MARK I. NICKERSON
AND
JOSHUA S. GOLDSTEIN

Skyhorse Publishing

Skyhorse Publishing books may be purchased in bulk at special discounts for sales promotion, corporate gifts, fund-raising, or educational purposes. Special editions can also be created to specifications. For details, contact the Special Sales Department, Skyhorse Publishing, 307 West 36th Street, 11th Floor, New York, NY 10018 or info@skyhorsepublishing.com.

Skyhorse® and Skyhorse Publishing® are registered trademarks of Skyhorse Publishing, Inc.®, a Delaware corporation.

Visit our website at www.skyhorsepublishing.com.

10 9 8 7 6 5 4 3 2 1

Library of Congress Cataloging-in-Publication Data is available on file.

Cover design by Brian Peterson
Cover photo credit AP Images

Print ISBN: 978-1-63220-419-6
Ebook ISBN: 978-1-63220-420-2

Printed in the United States of America

TO THE LUCEY FAMILY

CONTENTS

chapter 1

SAFE BUT NOT SOUND— RETURNING FROM WAR

JULY 14, 2003, was a beautiful, sunny day in New Haven, Connecticut. Down by the beach on Long Island Sound, hundreds of people filled a large parking lot at old Fort Nathan Hale, a colonial-era fort that had fallen into disrepair over the decades, found new life as a small museum, and now also served as a base for the U.S. Marine Corps Reserve and the Army National Guard.

The crowd had come to meet the members of the Marine Reserve 6th Motor Transport Battalion, Light Company, returning from Iraq. Many waved American flags and flags with the USMC logo in gold against a maroon background. Many carried balloons. Most were dressed informally, in shorts and skirts, tank tops and T-shirts. The colors sparkled in the sunshine.

One Mylar balloon with red and white stripes said simply, WELCOME HOME. One man's hat was made of red, white, and blue balloons that rose two feet above his head. A woman's top was fashioned like the American flag. Stars sat on her right shoulder; red and white stripes extended down her left side. A young child sat on her father's shoulder to get a better view. Every family seemed to have a camera, and many videotaped the festivities.

THE REUNION

The scene was reminiscent of the old Civil War song, "When Johnny Comes Marching Home Again," written by conductor Patrick Gilmore for his sister Annie to comfort her while her fiancé was away with the Union Army. "The men will cheer and the boys will shout; the ladies they will all turn out." It is a timeless scene, repeated after most of America's wars. Since that day in New Haven early in the Iraq War, it has been repeated countless more times as two and a half million Americans have returned from Iraq and Afghanistan.

At these homecomings, a feeling of hopefulness and relief enlivens the air. The civilians desperately want to believe that all is well, that order is restored. They want to "fill with joy the warrior's heart," as the song says, and to put war firmly behind them. But often the warriors themselves harbor ambivalence about such celebrations. While away, they have craved this homecoming and imagined it a certain way, yet when it actually happens, it feels different. In war they have seen, and perhaps done, terrible things—things that the happy men and ladies of the iconic song might never understand and, worse, might not really *want* to know about. Yes, the vets are home, but likely as not they have changed. The faces of their parents, siblings, lovers, and friends are familiar, but will these people understand or connect with the veterans? On the outside, of course, the returning heroes are all strength and smiles.

On that July day in New Haven, one particular family waited expectantly for their "Johnny." Their guy was Lance Corporal Jeffrey Lucey. His parents, Joyce and Kevin, were there to greet him, along with his sisters Debbie and Kelly, his girlfriend Julie, and family friends. Jeff's mother, Joyce, still recovering from a stroke she suffered while Jeff was away, was tired but eager. She had birthed this boy, raised him, seen him off to war, and couldn't wait to get him back. As the arrival was delayed, the family paced around the parking lot, looking at the ocean and waiting.

Jeff's father, Kevin, looked around and remembered how different the mood had felt the last time they were there. It had been a night of gloom and fear as Jeff's unit had slipped into the darkness at 4:00 AM to an uncertain war in a distant land. On this summer day, however, the moment was festive and bright. People laughed and chatted with glee, making instant friends with those around them.

The suspense continued as the buses were late. Word came that they had missed the exit but had turned around and were on their way back. Amidst the excitement, Kevin peered over the ocean and thought, "My God, everything looks so wonderful, peaceful, and beautiful. The world is coming back to us again."

Finally, there was a stirring in the crowd. The faint sound of sirens grew louder until everyone saw the police escort turn in with its lights flashing and sirens trumpeting. Then the first glimpse of the buses sparked a wave of excitement. The buses slowly pushed alongside the crowd, but the mob wouldn't allow them to go any further, and the Marines hurriedly disembarked. The crowd surged forward, clapping, cheering, and yelling. Everyone was looking for their Marine, and the Luceys found theirs.

Jeff looked great—tan, slender, smiling. He seemed surprised that so many people had come. Jeff said later that none of the Marines had expected the welcome home and the greeting that they received. Jeff was dressed in Marine fatigue camos, mostly sand-colored with swooshes of brown and green. LUCEY was printed on his right pocket and US MARINES on his left.

Jeff's girlfriend, Julie, carried an American flag and a bouquet of yellow and red flowers. They embraced, kissed, and then just gazed at each other, their noses touching, with the brim of Jeff's hat resting on Julie's head.

Kevin had been video recording the greetings. Now it was his turn, and he passed off the camera to his wife. Father and son embraced each other heartily. Jeff leaned his chin into his father's shoulder, holding on with his right hand squarely on his father's back. For several seconds, Kevin held his son firmly with both arms, his chin over Jeff's shoulder. Kevin was overwhelmed with joy and relief. He choked up as he whispered, "Welcome home, Jeff. Thank God, you are safe and sound."

A CALL FOR HELP

Nine months later, on April 29, 2004, I received a voicemail message at my psychotherapy practice, in the town of Amherst in western Massachusetts. I had been providing individual and family therapy in the community for many years and had helped many people address a broad range of issues that cause people to seek therapy.

The voicemail was from Joyce Lucey. "I think you probably remember my son, Jeffrey. You saw him when he was a teenager," it began. "We're wondering if you would be willing to see Jeffrey. He's really not doing very well, and he won't talk about it, but I think he's willing to see you." Jeff was living with his parents in the small town of Belchertown, Massachusetts, next to Amherst.

Joyce went on to explain that Jeff had served in Iraq, and on his return he seemed OK but had gotten "worse and worse" over the last few months. She and Kevin were "really worried about him." But they couldn't convince him to talk to anybody connected to the military. He was afraid it would only make his life worse if anyone in the military found out how much he was struggling.

Since I was a private therapist, our confidential sessions would not show up on his military service record. Joyce added, "He said he liked you when he saw you before and said he would see you again, but I'm not sure we can really get him to go."

I remembered Jeff pretty well. I had seen him about a dozen times when he was sixteen years old, eight years earlier. At that time, his grades had dropped, he was getting into mischief, and his parents had insisted he see a therapist. When we met for the first time, he agreed he wasn't taking his life very seriously. He continued to come in voluntarily, and we met periodically for about a year. He stayed out of any serious trouble, improved his grades, and seemed to be moving in a better direction.

This time around, his mother's brief message had an unmistakably anxious tone. I remembered her as a parent who loved her kids very much but tended to worry. Her words "not doing very well" didn't reveal much. Who is doing well when they call a therapist? I really didn't know what to expect, nor did I need to. As a seasoned therapist,

I like to think I am prepared to deal with whatever circumstances might come through my office door. For most therapists, it is gratifying to be able to assist someone effectively. It's especially satisfying when someone you've seen as a child or teenager remembers a strong enough positive connection to seek you out when he or she needs help years later. Even so, I wasn't sure if Jeff actually wanted to come in and talk with me or if he had just nodded his head when his parents said, "You've got to talk to somebody."

I called Joyce back. She offered a bit more detail, but I was hesitant to engage her in much conversation. I wanted to talk with Jeff directly, but he wasn't home. At the same time, I could sense her desperation, and I gave her a chance to share some of her concerns. Joyce sketched out Jeff's story for me. He had enlisted in the Marine Reserve, been called up for active duty and was part of the first wave of Marines that entered Iraq from Kuwait at the start of the war. He completed a six-month tour of duty and had seemed fine upon his return home the previous July. He had completed a semester at college that fall, even making the honor roll. He'd been living at home and, in his mother's words, didn't really do much other than go to school, but they figured he deserved the rest. Since Christmas, however, things had gone downhill. Joyce and Kevin didn't know what to do. They tried to get him to go to the VA hospital, but he wouldn't.

Normally I would ask that an adult "client" call me directly to set up the appointment, but in this case I heeded Joyce's words when she said, "I think we better just set a time, and then we'll try to get him to come to it." We scheduled for the next Monday. I was beginning to sense the depth of the Luceys' concerns and the hope they were placing in me that I might help their son.

That conversation signaled something atypical and compelling about what was to follow. Perhaps it was because Jeff and his family echoed back to an earlier phase in my career, and I was glad they valued me as a resource. Perhaps it was because I knew Kevin as a probation officer who had worked with some of my adolescent clients. Or perhaps it was because I sensed Joyce's urgency. But I also realized, as I prepared to see Jeff again, that this would be my first real contact with anyone returning from the Iraq War. The war was being fought by a thin slice of the American population, and the rest of us had little insight into what was going on over there.

That Monday morning, before the scheduled appointment, I decided to call the house to see if the appointment was still on. Jeff picked up the phone. "Hi Jeff, it's Mark Nickerson. I just thought I'd check to see if we are still on for 2:00."

"Oh," he responded. I could tell I had caught him off guard. "Oh, I meant to call you. Can we move the appointment to Friday? I'm really sorry. I meant to call you."

"OK, we can do that," I said, but as I hung up I wondered if I'd ever see Jeff. I resisted the temptation to call him during the week and was already imagining a conversation with Joyce about what they could do if he wouldn't come in. I was surprised when he showed up on time for the Friday appointment.

Initially, I was struck by how familiar Jeff seemed. Physically, he had filled out. As a teen, he had been a good-looking kid with an athletic body that he carried with a confident swagger. Now he was a bigger version of the same: chiseled features, square jaw, deep brown eyes, a friendly hello, and a solid handshake.

I smiled, invited him into my office from the waiting room, and we both sat down.

chapter 2

BRINGING THE WAR HOME— AMERICA'S POSTWAR PTSD PROBLEM

WHEN JEFF LUCEY walked into my office in 2004, the year after the invasion of Iraq, I was not yet prepared to deal with traumatized veterans returning from war, and neither was the rest of the country for that matter. Like most community-based therapists, I had never worked with a veteran who had just come back from the war zone, as the last such wave had ended in the 1970s after the Vietnam War. The Department of Veterans Affairs (VA), as it has since proven, was similarly unprepared for the wave of need that was about to hit its system. In 2004, Americans supported the War on Terror and did not anticipate its many costs.

In 2004, neither the public nor our political leaders could imagine that a decade later some two and a half million Americans would have served in Iraq and Afghanistan and that hundreds of thousands of them would suffer from post-traumatic stress disorder (PTSD).

AT WAR'S END

Yet here we are, at the end of another war, as the last American combat troops trickle back from Afghanistan in 2014. We can count the casualties from Iraq and Afghanistan. More than 6,000 U.S. personnel have been killed, and more than 50,000 have been wounded. Among the wounded are more than 1,500 amputees, nearly 7,000 veterans with the most severe, long-term forms of traumatic brain injury (TBI), more than 250,000 with mild concussions, and more than 300,000 with symptoms of PTSD.[1]

The VA, which has been charged with caring for these returning vets, has a backlog of cases that have been at a standstill for four months or longer—sometimes much longer. That's a long time for vets to wait to find whether they will get some kind of government assistance. And despite some progress on this waiting period in 2013, some 325,000 vets remained in the VA's backlog as of April 2014.[2]

In 2014 a scandal revealed widespread falsification of wait-time data for vets using VA services. VA administrators collected bonuses by reporting falsely that wait times were decreasing. Vets were dying while they waited for appointments. Secretary of Veterans Affairs Eric Shinseki resigned, and the government promised reform. The U.S. Congress, in a rare act of bipartisanship, passed additional funding for the VA. Time will tell if these measures have more success than past efforts.

A decade ago, as Jeff Lucey fell apart after returning from Iraq, nobody could conceive of what would unfold in the years to come. As it turned out, the Lucey family spent that next decade working to reform how America cares for its returning vets. I spent the same period advancing my skills with a powerful psychotherapy approach called Eye Movement Desensitization and Reprocessing (EMDR) and training other therapists to use it to treat vets with PTSD.

In the following chapters, I will take you through that decade by telling the story of what happened to Jeff, to the Luceys, and to me as a therapist. We will observe PTSD up close and understand how serious it can get. We will follow the family's journey as they worked to reform the government and change public consciousness about veterans and PTSD. We will follow my own journey as I learned the effective interventions for PTSD and began to promote their use in the mental health community. The book closes with thoughts about how to keep war veterans visible and supported as they reintegrate into civilian life.

But first, let me sketch the big picture as I have come to understand it. PTSD (which I will describe in more clinical terms in chapter 8) is a psychological condition caused by a terrifying experience that lodges in the brain as a raw memory, overwhelming the brain's usual processing system.[3] The frozen experience may manifest itself as nightmares, intrusive memories, or even hallucinations, and it often feeds related problems of substance abuse, sleep disorders, poor concentration, anger, relationship difficulties, and social isolation, among others. Of particular concern is the related issue of *suicidality*, a clinical term for the risk of attempting suicide. PTSD heightens the risk of suicide, although most PTSD sufferers do not take their own lives, and not all suicides occur along with PTSD.

THE SUICIDE FACTOR

In the later years of the war decade, as multiple deployments took their toll, suicide became a stark public marker of military PTSD. The pattern of increasing suicides was complex. Some of the victims had deployed and some had not; some were diagnosed with PTSD and some not; some died during active duty and others after returning to civilian life. But they all reinforced a picture of the U.S. military under stress after a decade at war.

The suicides generated media attention. A lone bugler against a gray sky filled the cover of *TIME Magazine* on July 23, 2012, above the headline ONE A DAY. By that point, America's rate of military suicides, outpacing the rate of combat fatalities, had passed the threshold of one daily among active-duty personnel. Among veterans (a much larger group including vets of earlier wars), the total number of suicides was nearly twenty times higher.[4]

The number of Americans who have taken their own lives after returning from Iraq or Afghanistan, however, is not easy to determine. The military tracks suicides of active-duty service members, running around one per day as of 2014, although the majority of those occurred in the United States, not overseas. The rate doubled over the last decade. The numbers for veterans are less clear. Of the twenty-two million living veterans from all eras, those returning from Iraq and Afghanistan make up about a tenth. Suicides from all veterans total about twenty a day, so possibly one or two per day would be vets from the wars in Iraq or Afghanistan. Finally, members of the Reserve and National Guard are taking their own lives at nearly the same rate as active-duty service members.

Put it all together, and it becomes clear that roughly a thousand Americans who served in Iraq or Afghanistan die by suicide every year bringing the total to about 5,000 to 10,000 Americans, a number that roughly equals the official U.S. war fatalities count of more than 6,000.

This suicide total does not count service members, reservists, and veterans who have died from drug overdoses, car accidents, or violence—any of which may or may not have been intentional—while suffering mental health problems after returning from the wars. For example, in November 2012, Jason Arsenault of Alabama, who had served two tours in Iraq and seen four buddies die when his helicopter was shot down, dressed up in his Army uniform and medals and then pointed an unloaded handgun at police, who killed him.[5] On the official record, he was considered neither a war death nor a suicide. Better data are needed because, as Army captain Brian Kinsella, the founding director of StopSoldierSuicide.org, puts it, "You can't manage what you can't measure."

The author of the Marine classic *Jarhead*, Anthony Swofford, took the military suicide issue to the pages of *Newsweek* and elsewhere.[6] Former Pentagon official Lawrence Korb addressed it in *Foreign Policy*.[7] Famed *New York Times* columnist Nicholas Kristof called out the VA, and the nation, on veterans' mental health and suicide issues.[8] And in an extraordinary move for an army still at war, on September 26, 2012, the U.S. Army held a one-day worldwide stand-down to deal with the suicide problem. "The nation has asked our soldiers to carry a heavy load over the last eleven years, and they have not failed," said the Army's top enlisted soldier. "But suicide is an enemy we have yet to defeat. . . . The Army has decided that this issue is so important to us that we're going to devote an entire day . . . that was otherwise devoted to something else and say 'That's not as important as this.'" Defense Secretary Leon Panetta underscored the point by instructing military commanders that "suicide prevention is a leadership responsibility" and telling them to "kick ass" to make changes.[9]

Since then the suicide rate has leveled off, but the big picture of caring for psychologically wounded veterans remains daunting.

PTSD IN HISTORY

The suicides may embody military PTSD in the public's eye, but America's PTSD problem is actually much broader and deeper. Throughout history, fighters have gone off to war, come home psychologically wounded, and suffered symptoms that we now call PTSD.

In the Civil War, a physician named Jacob Mendes Da Costa noted symptoms we recognize today as signs of psychological trauma. He used terms such as "irritable heart," "exhaustion," or more euphemistically, "soldier's heart" or "nostalgia" to describe his observations. Letters and diaries of Civil War soldiers show clear indications of PTSD.[10]

In World War I, the expanded use of heavy artillery led to the phrase "shell shocked" to describe those who couldn't get beyond the battlefield. Toward the end of the war, "war neurosis" became a common term. In World War II, terms such as "battle fatigue" and "old sergeant's syndrome" were used. The term PTSD was first used to describe some of the symptoms soldiers exhibited when they returned from the Vietnam War, and in 1980, it was added to the third edition of the *Diagnostic and Statistical Manual of Mental Disorders* (DSM-3).

Just as there is a history of soldiers going off to war, there is also a history of efforts to manage the effects of combat trauma on these soldiers. During World War I, World War II, and the Korean War, more men were pulled off the front lines because of psychological wounds than were killed in combat. Consequently, intervention strategies employed by the armed services evolved with each war.

Have we made progress in recognizing and treating military PTSD? Yes. In World War I, British psychiatrists considered "shell shock" a reflection of poor moral character, low self-discipline, or sheer cowardice. They treated traumatized soldiers with electric shocks and cigarette burns, yelled at them to "brace up," and sent them back to the front.[11] The idea of treating shell shock with respectful therapy instead of shame was a radical concept pioneered by the British doctor W. H. R. Rivers, whose most famous patient was Siegfried Sassoon, a World War I veteran who went on to write powerful poems about the horrors of war.

In World War II, after heavy fighting in Europe, as many as a quarter of the U.S. soldiers evacuated to medical facilities near the front were "uninjured physically but were babbling, crying, shaking, or stunned, unable to hear or talk." The Army gave them a day of rest and hot food, then sent three-quarters back to the front after one day and most of the rest after three days, with 10 percent unable to return to the front.[12]

After the Vietnam War, American mental health professionals coined the term PTSD and recognized it as a disability, but the Army also gave other than honorable discharges to soldiers suffering psychological breakdowns and denied them VA benefits.[13] Society as a whole did poorly in supporting returning vets from that war. Some young protesters even spat on them and called them "baby killers."[14] Soldiers faced additional forms of alienation as most tours of duty in Vietnam were solitary, individual episodes, especially for draftees. Rarely did whole units travel to the war zone together. Without unit integrity to buffer the individual against the overwhelming stresses of combat, Vietnam became a private war of survival for each American individual. The enemy was rarely uniformed, and there were no real lines of demarcation.

WHY THESE WARS ARE DIFFERENT

In some ways, America's most recent wars tell the same old story of military PTSD. But in other ways the problem has gotten worse. The nature of war has changed, with no clear front lines and with ever-present threats from improvised explosive devices (IEDs). As the VA's national director for readjustment counseling has put it, "This is urban warfare. There's no place to hide in Iraq. Whether you're driving a truck or you're a cook, everyone is exposed to extreme stress on a daily basis."[15]

The Iraq and Afghanistan wars were America's first major wars fought with an all-volunteer military consisting of only 1 percent of the population. That these wars were also unpopular politically further isolated returning troops from the civilian population, though not as badly as during Vietnam.

And in these two wars, more reservists and National Guard members were mobilized than ever before, leading to wrenching transitions from civilian to military life and back again. The maximum length of activation was increased from six months to twenty-four months. Employers are not required to pay Guard and Reserve members while they are deployed—just hold their jobs. Many faced cuts in pay, leading to financial hardships. The psychological transition home can be particularly abrupt for reservists and National Guard members, such as Jeff Lucey. After forming tight bonds with war buddies, the returning service member may feel isolated back at home in civilian life.

The wars dragged on for many years and forced multiple deployments. Troops no longer return home to stay after they have served. Instead, they shift back and forth in a grinding pattern of goodbyes and hellos, and families and children are put through the wringer with them each time. Communication technologies such as Skype, although welcome, stretch deployed troops in two directions. A deployed service member might have only a few hours between experiencing the violence of combat and talking with family.

Women in the military face additional challenges. They are much closer to combat now, must deal with shifting gender expectations, and not infrequently face (along with some men) violent sexual assault, known as Military Sexual Trauma (MST).

Advances in medical technology and body armor have meant that more injured troops survive. In World Wars I and II, wounded U.S.

troops outnumbered those killed by less than two to one. Today that ratio is around sixteen to one. Those exposed to battle are less likely to die, which is good news. But it also means that there's a higher percentage of physically wounded survivors than ever before.

Waiting and worrying back home, family members are aware of the inherent danger of military operations and the unknown factors of the post-9/11 world, and they are exposed to dramatic media reports. After the war, family members pick up the pieces and pay gargantuan costs (financial and personal) that, in all fairness, society as a whole should bear.

These issues are compounded by a longstanding culture of self-reliance and toughness within the military, with its stigma against seeking mental health help. As *Jarhead* author Anthony Swofford put it in 2012, service members think that "If you say, 'Hey, I need help,' that's like saying, 'I'm weak.'"[16]

Unlike in the Vietnam era, almost all Americans now express gratitude to veterans. But is that enough? *Thank You for Your Service* is the ironic title of journalist David Finkel's 2013 book, which is a devastating portrait of American soldiers and their families coping with loss and PTSD after returning from Iraq. For the veteran who doesn't have a job, has a marriage on the rocks, has been "backlogged" by the VA, and feels stigmatized and isolated from society, the message might sound more like, "Thank you for your service and good luck with those problems."

This is not to say that military and civilian groups are not making some progress in dealing with the tidal wave of returning vets with PTSD. First Lady Michelle Obama and Dr. Jill Biden have made military families a central concern. Many good efforts by nonprofit groups and many reforms by government agencies are underway. Indeed, some of these efforts (which I will describe later in the book) have grown out of the work of the Lucey family along with other advocates for veterans with PTSD and their families. All of these efforts are important foundations to build on as America attempts to care for its veterans with PTSD.

But still, with much of civilian society ignorant or uninterested in vets, and a VA system overwhelmed by the millions returning from thirteen years of war, America's military PTSD problem is undeniable, and it's still largely dumped in the laps of the veterans' families.

One of those families, one among the millions, was the Lucey family of Belchertown, Massachusetts.

chapter 3

"ENOUGH HORRIBLE THINGS TO LAST A LIFETIME"— JEFF IN IRAQ

JEFF'S CHILDHOOD NEITHER prepared him for military life nor deterred him from it. He seemed to be an average boy with a lot of energy, a charming smile, and a contagious laugh.

AN AMERICAN BOYHOOD

Jeff had a generally easygoing disposition, but when he did lose his temper as a child, his father would gather him up and lug him to his room where his anger would subside. Jeff loved to sit in his father's lap, drink his juice or milk, watch his cartoons, and then fall asleep. When Jeff was down or sulky, he typically kept to himself. Quietly, he would escape into his own mind and private activities. At some point, he would bounce back to his outgoing nature. His parents came to understand this process and how well it seemed to work for him.

Just as his older sister, Kelly, had looked after him, Jeff took seriously the responsibility of being an older brother to his other sister, Debbie. Even before Debbie started walking and talking, Jeff was there to guide her. Debbie, in turn, looked up to Jeff as her caretaker and protector. The family's strong bonds revealed themselves in particular each Christmas when they all piled in the car and made the rounds to visit Kevin and Joyce's extended families who lived in the surrounding towns.

Often, when Jeff found something that he truly cherished, he would bring it into bed with him. His parents remember that, when they were at Disney World, they bought their nine-year-old son a Davy Crockett rifle. Jeff was overwhelmed with joy. Back home, he would sleep with it in his sleeping bag.

Jeff loved that trip to Disney World. Unbeknownst to his parents, Jeff brought along some practical joke items to liven up the adventure. Both Snow White and Cinderella fell victim to Jeff's hand buzzer when he shook their oversized hands. The characters feigned shock, and everyone had a good laugh.

School interested Jeff mainly for the social aspect, though he did well in his schoolwork in elementary and middle school. One member of the Cub Scout den led by his parents on Tuesday afternoons was Pablo Chaverri, who would become Jeff's lifelong buddy despite their different family backgrounds (Pablo's parents came from Costa Rica). Jeff liked to play baseball, football, and basketball.

Jeff in 1991.

He was a decent pitcher and could sink a three-point shot with some consistency. He and his dad became fanatical baseball card collectors.

Jeff had a strong sense of loyalty, reinforced by his participation in the Cub Scouts and sports. He found like-minded friends and formed strong bonds with them. He and another friend, named Nick, were risk-takers and would do things like slide off the roof into snow banks. Not infrequently both boys' mothers were out searching for them. "Catch us if you can" was their philosophy.

As a teenager, Jeff took an interest in all-terrain vehicles (ATVs). He and Nick often drove off into the nearby woods. Most of their adventures centered on getting the ATVs unstuck and back out of the woods. Unfortunately, Jeff's expectations often exceeded what the ATVs could deliver, and given that neither Jeff nor his parents were mechanically inclined, the broken-down vehicles were sold as Jeff moved on to the next thing kids his age were doing.

Jeff had a serious side as well and earned the trust of many. When Jeff and his friend Nathan were twelve years old, Nathan's brother Raffie died. Soon after he heard the news, Jeff insisted on going over to Nathan's house. They went for a walk, and Jeff was able to comfort Nathan. When Jeff was fourteen years old, his grandfather, Kevin's dad, died suddenly of a heart attack. Jeff volunteered and was allowed to be a pallbearer. While he hadn't been particularly close to his grandfather, he felt the profoundness of the death.

Another time, when Joyce's father underwent open-heart surgery, Jeff asked to miss school to go with her to the hospital. When Shiloh, the family beagle, had seizures, Jeff would always take the dog outside and stand with him. "He wasn't one to shy away from problems," said his father. Kevin imagined Jeff's becoming a policeman or an EMT one day, someone who would not run away from an emergency but move toward it instead. When Jeff later decided to join the Marine Reserve to help disaster victims, his father wasn't surprised.

The Lucey family took others' difficulties seriously. Kevin volunteered a week of service each summer at Camp Sunshine in Sebago, Maine, a retreat for children with cancer and their families. The program was designed to lift the children's spirits and included many daily activities. Each year, one or more of the Lucey kids would join Kevin. One summer, Jeff and four or five others volunteered to form a Belchertown High School contingent that went to Camp Sunshine with Kevin for the week. The first day of the program, Jeff put on a Rocky Raccoon costume to entertain the families. He spotted a three-year-old girl dancing by herself and made his way, tail swaying, to dance with her. As it turned out, the girl had traveled to the camp from a town near Belchertown. When Jeff later found out that she died soon after from cancer, he talked about it with his parents with great concern.

When Jeff was about fifteen years old, Kevin used to take him to Dunkin' Donuts to buy them each a coffee. French Vanilla was Jeff's favorite. This became a father-son ritual. They often took their coffee and headed off to the Quabbin Reservoir. The Quabbin had been created in the 1930s to hold the 400 billion gallons of water that supplied Boston some sixty-five miles away. It is a beautiful setting with a twenty-mile-long lake surrounded by protected woodlands. A few service roads meander around its southernmost point.

Kevin and Jeff enjoyed the connection they felt in this timeless retreat away from life as usual. On these secluded roads, Kevin first gave his son the chance to drive, unbeknownst to Joyce. They would laugh while Jeff adeptly steered the car with one hand and held his coffee with the other. He drove quite well and didn't seem to notice that they were traveling at 15 mph tops. During these trips, he and his dad felt free to talk about anything.

New challenges came, however, with Jeff's mid-teen years. In high school he was bright enough but didn't make the effort to be a good student. He did very little homework and got by on what he picked up in class and could show on a test. His friends were still his primary focus. He distanced from his parents, as adolescents often do, and would sneak out of his bedroom window after his parents were asleep on weekend nights to meet up with his buddy Pablo for a night of adventure. Jeff had a strong drive to explore. More than once, Joyce discovered Jeff's empty bed after midnight and drove around until she located the boys. Joyce was frustrated by these changes in Jeff, but Kevin had more of a laissez-faire attitude. "He'll come back home when he's tired," Kevin would say.

Meanwhile, Jeff had some disappointing sports experiences. He didn't make the high school baseball team, and three bouts of pneumonia hurt his athletic abilities. His relationships within his peer group began to shift. He started going to parties. Other kids would call him goody-goody because his dad was a probation officer, and so, being an adolescent, Jeff had to prove he was one of the gang. One October day, shortly after he got his driver's license, Jeff, along with a group of teenagers and a case of beer, was headed for a party. The car veered onto the shoulder of the road, Jeff lost control of the wheel, and they collided with a stone wall. Nobody was hurt, but it was around this time that his parents referred him for counseling. Soon after the accident, Jeff became enamored of a girl named Julie. They just seemed to fit from the start, and became a well-liked couple among their friends. Their parents communicated regularly and welcomed Jeff and Julie into each other's homes.

Jeff and Pablo at high school graduation, 1999.

Late in his junior year of high school, a light seemed to go on, and suddenly Jeff became more concerned about the future. His grades improved, he had his own car, and he began working in retail stores. During his senior year he realized college was important. He applied himself and earned A's. At his high school graduation in June 1999, he exuded pride in his accomplishments and talked about his plans for the future. He was accepted at Holyoke Community College, where he planned to focus on business or possibly law enforcement. He remained connected to Julie as well as his childhood buddies, Pablo, Nathan, Nick, and the others. He was ready to grow up, develop self-discipline, and move forward with his education and career. He also wanted to do something honorable and make a difference in the world. To Jeff, joining the Marine Reserve made a lot of sense. His parents were not so sure about it, though.

"JUST DON'T SIGN ANYTHING"

The Marines had been interested in Jeff and Pablo for a while. Recruiters had come to Belchertown High School to build relationships and drum up interest. Then in August 1999, shortly after Jeff graduated from high school, a young man visited Jeff's house. He was dressed sharply in a United States Marine Corps uniform. He said he'd been sent by someone Jeff knew from high school, a boy a year older who had joined the Marine Reserve right after graduation and had already completed boot camp. Jeff and Pablo viewed him differently than other high school friends because he had done something with his life.

Soon after, Jeff and Pablo met with the recruiter. This was followed by numerous phone calls, so persistent that at times Jeff asked his parents to tell the recruiter he wasn't there. Pablo remembers all the phone calls as "very persistent, and from different people." Joyce remembers the recruiter from the few interactions they had as "a smooth talker and very, very persistent." Kevin was concerned about the recruiter's hard-sell but his overarching principle, learned from his own father, was to let Jeff make his own decisions. Like many people his age, Jeff didn't feel that he had a specific direction in life. High school was behind him, and he wasn't going away to a four-year college like some of his friends. Community college was in his sights, but that plan would mean continuing to live at home and commuting. He was restless and aimless, looking for adventure.

What mattered most to Jeff was his relationship with Julie. They had been together for two years. She was his first and only serious relationship. They were sweethearts, and people assumed that they would get married someday. Julie gave Jeff's life meaning. With her in mind, Jeff realized that he wanted to establish himself as an adult and earn a good income so that he could give her the lifestyle that he thought she would want. Though he had held a few jobs in retail and telemarketing, his career prospects did not seem great.

Money concerns loomed large for Jeff. He and Pablo were running out of ideas of places to look for work. One day, their job search brought them to the headquarters of the Quabbin Reservoir, looking for an outdoor job. Again, no openings. They lingered on the Quabbin grounds at the top of a hill and gazed across the vast, deep reservoir as they discussed their options. "The Marines—should we do this?" Pablo and Jeff pondered the pros and cons of joining. They figured it might be their best plan.

On December 6, 1999, Jeff came home and told his parents that a Marine Corps recruiter was going to take him and Pablo overnight to a motel. Kevin and Joyce didn't want their son to make any major decision without looking at all sides. They knew that Jeff was eighteen and free to make his own decisions, but he was fresh out of high school. They did not like the idea that a recruiter would take him away from his support system to a detached setting, out of view of his parents. Still, they didn't put up a fight, and after a brief discussion, Pablo and Jeff left.

"Just don't sign anything," Jeff's father had said. "Whatever the recruiter says, come back and we can discuss the pros and cons."

When Jeff and Pablo returned the next morning, they had signed up.

The motel was the Comfort Inn in Chicopee, a nearby small city best known for its air base with C5-A Galaxy cargo jets, the largest in the fleet. Pablo said years later, "The recruiters are salesmen; they say whatever it takes for you to buy in." The recruiters took out a set of cards with different words on them, such as DISCIPLINE, GET IN SHAPE, MONEY, SKILLS, and LEARNING. They laid the cards out on the motel bed, and one recruiter asked, "Which one makes the most sense to you? What do you want for your life?" Pablo recalled the approach as simple, direct, and concrete. "Then the recruiter would explain how you could get that if you join the Marines. They gave examples, like of a kid who would never clean his room. After boot camp, his bed was made." The recruiters offered a rite of passage to a meaningful grown-up life. Pablo himself wanted to get in shape. He was prone to carrying extra weight, and the thought that the Marines could help him buff up was quite appealing. In fact, he said, "I was over the weight limit at the time, but they said 'sign up anyways and we will work with you.'" Whatever it took to get them in the door.

Pablo remembers that nowhere in the recruitment process was there any discussion about the recruit's readiness to meet the real challenges that might lie ahead. Boot camp was touted much more as a pathway to becoming a man (or woman) than as preparation for real combat. To make it through boot camp was a true test of one's mettle and something the Marine could be proud of forever. Six weeks to adulthood. Actually, it didn't seem like that much. According to Pablo, the recruitment included no psychological testing and no hard questions to determine whether the recruit was actually a good fit for military service. "It was more about getting us to sign."

The Reserve had a particular appeal, seeming to offer the best of both worlds, military and civilian. Jeff and Pablo learned that the reservists and the active-duty Marines went to the same boot camp, but the active-duty Marines became full-time. The reservists served one weekend a month, two weeks each summer, and were available if needed for active duty.

When Jeff returned home the next morning, having signed the papers, his parents were shocked, but attempted to be as supportive as possible. Jeff was excited and told his father he was preparing for the future, school, and a career. And he talked about "the brotherhood" of the Marines. Sensing his parents' reserved response, Jeff added, "But understand, Dad, that we can help people. When there are disasters in the country, the National Guard and reservists get called in. We'll be helping people."

When Jeff's parents mentioned that he had agreed with them not to sign anything, he explained that they shouldn't worry; he and Pablo would not actually start until they had completed their fall and spring semester at community college. This must have seemed like a safe enough distance away to Jeff, but to his parents it seemed just around the corner. Pablo remembers the decision felt like "somewhat of a free choice because I had known previously of someone who signed but didn't end up going. I forgot how he did it; he had to go in front of someone. So, I felt safe signing." Pablo was correct, although rarely are recruits informed that they can opt out any time before they are sworn in. Even if they knew their choices, most recruits would avoid the stigma and sense of failure that would likely come with requesting a withdrawal.

Jeff spoke to his parents about the money he would make and how his school costs would be paid. He went on about all the benefits the recruiter had discussed, like retirement, the brotherhood, the sense of accomplishment, the savings, and the G.I. Bill. Jeff looked at it as being beneficial for Julie and him once they started a family.

As excited as Jeff was about enlisting, as May of 2000 drew closer, he grew more apprehensive and nervous. Kevin reasoned to himself that since 1991 there had been peace, and there were no apparent military threats looming on the horizon. Jeff was going into the Reserve, not the active-duty Marines. Kevin got more comfortable with the notion that Jeff was enlisting to try to help people in national disasters and calamities. He and Joyce were pleased that their son was thinking about his future.

BOOT CAMP AND BEYOND

Right from the start, Pablo remembers the deal changing. "We were supposed to be on the delayed entry program. Attend boot camp, come home, and go to school. But we got screwed and ended up having to go through boot camp and then having to go right away. There was nothing I could do about it. When I found out, I said to the drill instructor, 'Sir, this recruit needs to speak, Sir.' But he said, 'No, this is what you got, it says it right here.'"

A shadow fell as Jeff's date with boot camp approached. Jeff's parents remember being aware of each moment as the days slipped by and they moved toward the unknown. But they were trying to enjoy the time as well. It was the beginning of living a double life, the pretense of normal with undercurrents of worry—the life of a military family.

Their friends threw Jeff and Pablo a going-away party that included his family, grandparents, and Julie. But Jeff's parents had noticed a darkening of his mood, with his jovial laughter becoming less frequent. The night before Jeff was scheduled to be picked up, he packed and waited nervously. The phone rang, and the caller told him that he would not be leaving that day. "Tomorrow," the caller said. Jeff appeared both relieved and disappointed at the same time.

The next day, Jeff went off only to meet with more confusion. At a meeting he learned that the plan to attend boot camp and return to finish college, an option that had been promised to him, wouldn't be available. So Jeff returned home. He had been given a couple of hours to decide whether to stay in or drop out. Jeff and his parents talked it over. His parents tried not to influence his decision but instead to describe all the pros and the cons they could think of. When the recruiter came back, Jeff went with him.

The recruiter had raised Jeff's hopes about the amount of money that he would have after boot camp, but failed to tell him that he would be responsible for many costs, such as for uniforms and equipment. Jeff felt deceived when he learned this during boot camp.

Shortly after the recruits got off the bus, the drill instructor addressed everyone and demanded to know who "Lucy" was. Jeff identified himself, and the instructor ridiculed him in front of all the others. He said he was not going to have a person called "Lucy," a girl's name, graduate from his unit. Jeff was uneasy about the demeaning attitude toward women expressed by the drill instructor and some of the other recruits. For a while, Jeff continued to be taunted by the drill instructor. From that point on, he didn't want to be singled out at all, for negative or positive reasons. Jeff later told his parents about the physical abuse that went on. Once when Jeff was ironing his clothes, the drill instructor shoved him over the ironing board for no apparent reason. Sometimes at night the drill instructor would shine a flashlight in someone's face and take him outside to do exercises. Jeff thought that was against procedures, but he kept his mouth shut and did what he was told. He noticed that others got it "pretty bad," especially the "fat bodies" (as Marines traditionally refer to their overweight colleagues).

In one letter, Jeff wrote, "I walked into the bathroom with about ten other guys today to find a recruit with his wrists slit on the ground unconscious. He had also drank some rubbing alcohol and there has been no word on his condition." He later remarked that when the drill instructor arrived, he verbally lashed the young man for what he'd done. They never saw the recruit again. Jeff learned to obey and be as invisible as possible as part of his just-survive strategy for boot camp.

Jeff's letters home included some initial comments about his adjustment. "They haven't even let us shower in three days. We have to wake up at four. I could really use a cigarette. The food is horrible. I'm so homesick." Later he tempered his complaints—"I don't want you to worry about me. I'm going to be fine"—but said he was sleep-deprived.

Jeff dreaded in particular a challenge known as "The Crucible," which required staying awake for forty-eight hours straight and trying to overcome the obstacles and achieve the tasks that were placed before him. However, after he successfully completed The Crucible, Jeff began to reflect more confidence and optimism. He was over a hump. Kevin, Joyce, Debbie, and Julie flew from Boston to Savannah, Georgia, to attend his graduation. They found Jeff thinner, well-tanned, and happy to see them.

During boot camp, Jeff discovered that the recruiter had not done the work he had promised. He was supposed to have obtained Jeff's college records and processed them, which would assure that Jeff would graduate from boot camp as a Private First Class. Jeff wrote his parents imploring them to ask the recruiter to take care of this. After no response from the recruiter, Kevin took it upon himself to go to the college, get Jeff's transcript, and drive it to the recruiting office at the

Kevin, Jeff, and Joyce at Parris Island, 2000.

Federal Building. Despite this, the papers weren't processed, and Jeff graduated as a Private, the lowest rank. This was later amended, but it was another scratch on the recruiter's glossy promises.

Due to the retracted promise of Deferred Entry to his second level of training, Jeff had only ten days at home before he was scheduled to head to Camp Lejeune, North Carolina, for ten weeks of training in a Military Occupational Specialty (MOS). He spent most of that time with Julie.

Jeff enjoyed his stay at Camp Lejeune more than Parris Island, and the ten weeks passed like the snap of a finger. During his training (as an administrative assistant), Jeff was asked to consider serving as a guard at the White House or embassies. He had an opportunity to receive special training in Washington, DC. The only hitch was that he would have to become an active Marine to qualify. He was worried, though, that if he didn't qualify, he'd have committed himself to four years of unknown duties. Although he had received the highest physical fitness and academic scores in training, he didn't want to take the risk. After all, he had been misled before. When he returned home, he was assigned to the 6th Motor Transport Battalion stationed in New Haven, Connecticut, about a ninety-minute drive from Belchertown.

AFTER 9/11

On September 11, 2001, Joyce and Kevin were at home and watched the horrifying news unfold on their television screen. The United States was under attack. Jeff returned from Julie's abuzz with what was going on. Jeff told his parents that this was going to affect him and his unit. He wanted to be activated and go to New York to assist in the recovery efforts or to go after the people who had done this. The Luceys thought about the decade of peace the country had enjoyed before Jeff joined and how that had changed in mere moments. Fear and apprehension had replaced calm. Jeff's unit was not sent to New York to help but began preparing for the possibility of war in Afghanistan.

Instead, they and the country abruptly took a different direction. National and international debates shifted from al Qaeda and its Afghanistan hosts, the Taliban, to Iraq and the danger posed by its weapons of mass destruction. Unlike the war in Afghanistan, the international community was divided about attacking Iraq, and many U.S. allies opposed it. Jeff and Pablo did not understand the new focus on Iraq. It didn't make sense to them. They wanted to go to Afghanistan. While some in Jeff's unit were "gung ho" for action, others didn't agree with the direction the government was taking.

Jeff's weekend trainings changed to include preparation for chemical, biological, and nuclear weapons. He learned about the impact of exposure and the horrible effects that the gasses could have on the person exposed to them. Gas masks had to be on within nine seconds to survive.

Christmas was bittersweet in 2002. The war drums were beating louder. One could sense that the nation's leaders had decided what they wanted to do. In the patriotic fervor after 9/11, few in Congress questioned the military attack. Jeff was given papers to sign for the power of attorney and his last will and testament. It all seemed surreal.

In January 2003 Jeff prepared all of his gear and spent his last evening at Julie's. Everyone tried to get some rest, but nobody could. Kevin and Joyce left home at 1:40 AM in the pitch dark, picked up Jeff in uniform with his gear, and drove him mostly in silence to report to his base at 4:00 AM. Kevin's mood matched the sky outside—no moon, stars, nothing, just vast emptiness. He wondered if this would be the last time he would see Jeff. What would Jeff experience? Why hadn't they tried to talk him out of joining? He thought of Jeff as the little boy sitting on his lap, rocking him to sleep, looking for baseball cards, and going to Disney World. Jeff and his clownish ways. In the back seat, Jeff rested his head against Julie as they drove through the night.

At the base, they all put on a good face. Through the darkness pierced only by the street lights they could see cars lined up and down both sides of the street. Families were standing with their Marines, unloading gear, and saying their goodbyes. The Luceys got out of the car, made small talk, gave reassurances, and hugged Jeff. Kevin told Jeff that everything would be OK and he would be back home soon. Jeff gathered up his gear and walked dutifully away. Kevin lingered to watch as Jeff was swallowed up by the darkness. Other Marines called out his name and joined him as they all disappeared into a building. The family stood there, still gazing after him. They drove home mostly in silence, wrapped up in their own thoughts and wondering if they would see Jeff alive again. Kevin would recall it as a "surreal experience, knowing that the child you protected all his life and whom you brought up not to hurt others and to be sensitive to others, that your child now was going to be immersed in all the dangers, chaos, and horrors of war."

OFF TO WAR

Jeff's unit took buses to the airport, a plane to Camp Pendleton in California, and a twenty-two-hour flight through Germany to Kuwait, where they arrived at 3:30 AM, moved out in a convoy of thirty

Humvees two hours later, arrived in a huge sandstorm, and slept on the floor that night. During this transition starting in February 2003, Jeff's parents didn't hear much from him. He sent home his civilian clothes and his ATM card. In Kuwait, Jeff and Pablo were sent to different places and didn't see each other until later in the deployment.

In Kuwait, Jeff began a journal on a small spiral-bound pad. He recorded his feelings and reflections until the day they crossed into Iraq. During the buildup, Jeff noted a mixture of boredom and apprehension. The Marines would play games to while away the time. Jeffrey wrote home occasionally and made a few calls. His family, like many other families and organizations, sent care packages regularly. They included magazines, hard candies, and cleaning wipes, anything that might make him more comfortable. Jeff received a card and a small package from one of the elementary school classes from Belchertown. He also received a few letters from people with whom Joyce worked at the nursing home. And he actually responded to them, to their surprise and delight.

In his journal, Jeff described the appalling sanitary conditions the 6th Motors encountered in Kuwait—"crippled toilets which were always full of waste all the way to the toilet seat was the only available toilets besides digging a cat hole in the desert." The troops "were being served some hot chow which was horrible for about a week but after a couple of food poisoning incidents, MREs [Meals Ready to Eat] became the only source of food. Water was rationed to 1.5 liters per day." Activities were random, with the Marines sometimes unpredictably pulled from their beds to work. Sleep deprivation was a constant.

But then they moved to an Army camp that they named "Camp Paradise." Jeff wrote that this camp had a "very nice chow hall which even serve[s] steak and lobster every other Saturday along with good filling meals three times a day. They have full showers that even had curtains to provide you with some privacy as you bathe. And to top it off, which amazes us probably the most was the flushing toilets." (What they actually got there was at least one good meal a day, no water rations, and a five-minute shower every other day.) During their time in Kuwait, "every now and again we would get a hold of a football or soccer ball or baseball with gloves and a bat. We would play in the middle of the desert under the hot sun like third graders during recess on the schoolyard. During this time we felt free, completely forgetting our surrounding environment. To work out we would run for miles usually before the hot West Asian sun would rise. We had some weights to lift and what we didn't have we made."

The unit went to the port to unload vehicles from huge cargo ships, each holding a thousand vehicles. The buildup to the war was one of the largest military logistical movements in history. Jeff and the others worked at this from early February until March 21, 2003.

On March 8, Jeff wrote in his notebook:

It is our 53rd day of Activation and we've been in country for four weeks to the day. I decided to wait this long before writing because I wanted to wait for most of my emotions to be drained from my system to make this an accurate account of our hour to hour, day to day, week to week ventures. Emotions such as anger towards our anything but wise commander in chief for ripping us out of our daily lives and pasting us into a waste depository named Kuwait, or pain and heartache from missing the loved ones we left behind and of course the depression that forms when these two emotions are mixed together. With the deep thought associated with depression blooms uncertainty. Uncertainty can drive any man crazy, the uncertainty about what's going to change about your life upon your arrival home. Will all your loved ones still be there? Was your significant other loving only you while you were 8 thousand miles away? . . . And will your friends and loved ones be the same people or will they have evolved into people you no longer know. Most importantly will we be the same when you get back or will we have changed ourselves and if we do, will we know that we changed or force blame for the changes on the home environment?

On March 18, Jeff turned twenty-two years old. The next day, the war began. On the second day, Jeff wrote in his notebook:

At 10:30 PM a SCUD [missile] landed in our vicinity. We were just falling asleep when a shockwave rattled through our tent. The noise was just short of blowing out your eardrums. Everyone's heart truly skipped a beat and the reality of where we are and what's truly happening hit home. It's now 11:30 and we still have no word of casualties but from the power encompassed in that blast the fear of the worst for many is very real. We are now trying to go to sleep for at least a couple of hours but anxiety is high and sleep seems close to impossible. A friend named Hazel who was in the rack beside me was looking at his three-month-old baby boy when the SCUD hit. When he came in he picked up the picture off the floor and gave me a look that seemed to say I hope I will hold him again. We now just had a gas alert and it is past midnight. We will not sleep. Nerves are on edge.

Jeff stopped writing in his journal, and the story of what happened to him in Iraq is fragmentary, gleaned from what he revealed in pieces to people back home and through the recollections of his unit's members as told afterwards to others, including journalists and the Marine Corps. Though his Reserve unit deployed together, its 183 members were often separated and assigned in different locations. In the early days of the war there were no opportunities for email, Skype, or cell phone calls.

Jeff deployed in Kuwait or Iraq, 2003.

BUMPS IN THE ROAD

The 6th Motors were part of the big push northward over the border from Kuwait into Iraq. Jeff's primary duty was as a truck driver. For a period, he drove a Humvee with a .50-caliber machine gun mounted on it. He reported driving during the night with the lights off and seeing fires in the distance. He learned to keep close behind the truck in front of him lest he get lost, which would be a potentially fatal mistake. At times, though, he drove the lead truck and felt the weight of responsibility for the lives of those in the trucks behind him.

The dangers of getting lost were quite real. A few days into the war, as part of the same push into the south of Iraq, an Army convoy of eighteen vehicles with thirty-three soldiers, very similar to the convoys Jeff drove in for the Marines, took a wrong turn. One hour later, trying to retrace its steps to the correct route, the convoy came under heavy attack resulting in the loss of eleven American lives (including the first female casualty), fifteen of the vehicles, and a number of Americans taken prisoner.

Other anxieties included the fear of incoming SCUD missiles and the dread of facing chemical gasses. Pablo recalls the SCUDs as the worst thing he faced in Iraq. "They were pretty crazy." And putting on protective suits in the scorching heat was "scary."

Jeff evidently found the first days of the war traumatic. He was part of a massive invasion of a hostile country. The mission was to destroy the Iraqi army, get to Baghdad, and overthrow the government—not to make friends along the way.

The order to Jeff and the other drivers was to push ahead, not to stop for anything no matter what, and "just don't look back." Jeff later described how kids would come running up to the trucks looking for candy, but he was instructed that this could be a ploy to stop the convoy so it could be ambushed. Jeff was troubled by what he called the "bumps in the road." The truck drivers were left to wonder if they had hit a pothole, knocked a goat out of the way, or run over a five-year-old child. There was no way to know, and the order was to keep moving, full speed. To do otherwise could put at risk the lives of the Marines he was carrying. A reporter later quoted Jeff's sergeant as saying, "The convoy commanders were explicit: 'Hit 'em. Crush 'em.' One driver in the unit did hit a man who got too close. No one knows if he survived. 'You don't look back,' a fellow Marine explained."[17] In this war, even a reservist truck driver had to make instantaneous choices that could mean life or death for fellow Marines and Iraqi civilians alike.

The official Marines account stated that Jeff's transport unit sustained no injuries from enemy action during its deployment and received only "sporadic, ineffective small arms fire" which they "seldom" returned. But a journalist reported that north of the Kuwait border "convoys were stoned; trucks were surrounded by angry Iraqis. The level of fear was always high as the drivers of the seven-ton trucks steered their way through the dusty streets of Safwan."[18]

Jeff also told his family of the sleep deprivation, the lack of water, the lack of food during the early stages of the invasion, and of the continued fear, stress, and insecurity. He reported seeing an Iraqi family killed as they were trying to get back to their house. He spoke of burying bodies and body parts, and of cleaning blood from the sand before the press arrived after an incident.

TRANSPORTING PRISONERS

One task that fell to Jeff's unit was to transport Iraqi prisoners of war (POWs), large numbers of whom had surrendered as the American forces advanced, yet not all of them were cooperative. As a sergeant in Jeff's unit later described it, "I never saw any prisoners get beat, but they weren't treated the best. Did I shove people and scream at people for absolutely no reason? Yeah. Did I really, really hurt anybody? No. But . . . I didn't think of them as human anymore. They were more like cattle."[19] However, Jeff and some of the other drivers sometimes shared their food or water with the POWs, who would tell stories of being drafted into Saddam Hussein's army on the threat of having their family members killed one by one if they didn't cooperate.

One time Jeff's fellow Marines called him over to show off a POW they had hog-tied with a sack over his head. The prisoner was trying to stay balanced in a squatting position with his hands tied behind him.

Jeff took a photo of the scene. According to another Marine who was there, Jeff did not feel right about what they were doing.

On another occasion, Jeff was reunited with Pablo, and they were assigned to transport some prisoners. One prisoner had concealed a razor blade and had cut through his zip-tie handcuffs. When Jeff stopped the truck to relieve himself, the prisoner went for Pablo's throat with the razor blade. Pablo blocked the attack but was gashed across the forearm. Jeff ran back to help subdue the prisoner and was alarmed by the amount of blood flowing from Pablo's arm. The episode ended "very badly" for the prisoner. This was as much detail as Jeff would tell his sister, other than that his adrenaline was pumping, that people had to act quickly in these situations, and that he wished he could erase the whole experience.

THE FOLKS BACK HOME

Back in the United States, the Luceys were handling things in their own individual ways. Kevin, who had been a news addict in the past, now hardly watched the news at all. Rather, he would pick up bits of information from newspapers, where it seemed a little less real. On the other hand, Joyce had as many as three televisions at a time tuned to various news channels in different rooms of the house. She hoped to get a glimpse of Jeff or hear about his unit.

Jeff's parents grew edgier as the days passed. Their swirling fear and helplessness would spike every time an injury or death was announced. They wondered how they had been able to distance themselves from the reports of dead and wounded in past wars.

As time went on, Joyce increasingly monitored the news for casualties. When she heard that a Marine had died, a twelve-hour clock in her head started ticking. The Luceys had the impression that it would take up to twelve hours for a family to be notified after their Marine had died. So for the next twelve hours, Joyce would try to calm her dread as she half-expected a strange car to pull into the driveway. With the release of the name or after the twelve-hour wait was up, there was relief, yet the relief would soon be replaced by guilt. The Luceys realized that if it wasn't Jeff, then some other family's world had just been shattered.

When someone back home received a letter from Jeff, calls went out to let everyone know. Sometimes Jeff would put a number of letters in the same envelope to be distributed. As they learned later, the content of the letters would be tailored to the recipient. To his parents, he said that all was mostly OK. To his sisters, Debbie and Kelly, he was reassuring but would give a little more information. To Julie, his girlfriend, he would write more candidly about his deeper concerns, including doing immoral things, things that he thought existed only in the movies, things he wished he could forget.

During this time, Joyce had been feeling fatigued and was having headaches, which were getting worse. Her doctor ordered an MRI. The results indicated that she had suffered a stroke. No doubt, the stress of the past months had taken a toll.

NASIRIYAH

The most intense period for Jeff's unit came early in the war as the Marines moving northward attacked the Iraqi town of Nasiriyah on the Euphrates River in late March 2003. This was the biggest and deadliest battle for the Marines, with eighteen of them killed on March 23 alone. The Nasiriyah period was chaotic. Spontaneous convoys would form and need drivers. Jeff's unit leaders would ask for volunteers. Everyone volunteered so as not to look bad in front of the others. Pretty soon the unit members were dispersed up and down the Euphrates. In Jeff's unit, drivers were assigned to different units, including to the 24th Marine Expeditionary Unit (MEU), a special-operations-capable force fighting in Nasiriyah. They were called back in to some cities that had already been cleared by the Marines. In these cases the Marines had an understanding that "all rules of engagement are off—shoot anything that moves," as Jeff would later recall.

What part Jeff played during the battle is unclear, as it is hard to say even where he was during that period. He only partially referred to his activities in letters or later in person. So his story is incomplete, not unlike many accounts of war. "We know *something* happened to Jeff over there," his father would later say. "Nobody will ever completely know. Things happened that changed him; it doesn't necessarily matter what happened."

The night before moving out with the 24th, Jeff wrote a love letter to Julie and tucked it into a calendar where it could be found if need be. "Baby, if you have this letter, I am no longer around." In another letter a few weeks later, he referred to that stashed-away letter: "I wrote that the night before we went into Nazariah with the 24th Marine Expeditionary Unit . . . We knew when we were told that we were going with them it was going to be really dangerous so I wanted that letter written and I wanted you to know where it was. But we did a lot of risky missions that would take me a whole notebook to write about. So I'll just wait till I get home."

A member of Jeff's unit, Mike Wetherbee, later recalled that in this period convoys typically came under fire once or twice per trip. Contrary to the regular procedure of assigning two 6th Motors drivers per truck, Wetherbee said, the unit was stretched thin, and Jeff would have been mostly driving alone. Wetherbee drove two missions with Jeff that transported prisoners. One journalist said of the Nasiriyah battle, "They talked about truck drivers who took up rifles and joined the 'grunts,' going house to house looking for Iraqi forces, providing cover for the grunts, fighting back—and taking prisoners. Wetherbee was pretty sure Jeff had been a part of that mission."[20] Although Jeff was a truck driver, the Marine tradition is "Every Marine a rifleman." In other words, whatever your specialty, you'd better be ready to shoot if called upon.

After the Nasiriyah period, Jeff sent Julie a small American flag with blood stains on it. He wrote, "When I get home, I'll explain the story about the flag." As that story came out later, again in fragments, Jeff reported that on one occasion, he saw a boy lying on the edge of a street dead but clutching the small flag. Jeff pulled the boy's body fully to the side and took the flag. After coming home from the war, Jeff treated the flag with special respect. He told his mother later that he had tried to wash out the blood but was unsuccessful.

After returning home, Jeff referenced one other significant incident during this Nasiriyah period. Once again, Jeff's description came out in fragmented though highly emotional remarks he made on separate occasions to his sister, father, a friend, a Vietnam vet, and to me, his therapist. Each person indicated to me that he or she didn't probe Jeff for information beyond what he volunteered, as the focus was on letting him speak freely. Hence, I have threaded together the following brief synopsis.

At some point during these complex and sometimes chaotic operations, Jeff reported that he was driving with at least one other Marine, who was his superior, and they came upon two suspicious Iraqi men by the road in a remote area. Jeff's superior apparently decided that the men were dangerous and ordered Jeff to shoot them at close range.

As Jeff later confessed, he stood there facing the two men with his gun shaking. They were about Jeff's age, and he thought to himself that they could be someone's son, brother, or perhaps father. A voice behind him said, "Pull the fuckin' trigger, Lucey." Jeff would later recall the closeness of the shooting, the loud sound, and the blood. Back home, Jeff would keep two dog tags on him constantly and said they were from the two men he'd killed.

In mid-April, Jeff wrote to Julie, "I would never want to fight in a war again. I've seen and done enough horrible things to last a lifetime. I never thought that outside of the movie theater I would see what I have seen. But I did—and I'm going to be able to see normal life again and best of all you." On April 18, he wrote her, "I have done so much immoral s**t during the last month that life is never going to seem the same, and all I want is to erase the past month, pretend it didn't happen."

WINDING DOWN

Jeff's tone with his parents, however, was more reassuring. On April 16, 2003, Jeff wrote his parents:

> *I'm just writing to tell you that it's pretty much over and I'm still alive and well although I'd just about give my soul for a shower and a nice cold drink. I also lost a little weight, actually more than a little. During the war food, water, and sleep were pretty hard to*

come by. . . . We are not even positive that the war is over although we think so since we haven't been running many missions for like a week now. All the guys really want to go home. Morale has really hit an all time low and sandstorms are getting ridiculous. Oh, yeah, by the way I was looking through that Sports Illustrated *you sent me and I saw some cool sunglasses that I want to order. I don't have my debit card with me so I sent the order form with this letter to you. I hope it reaches you in time because the offer is only good until June 30th . . ."*

Jeff seemed ready to step back into home life.

Two weeks later, he wrote again:

I'm still in Iraq but we're hoping to be back to Kuwait within two weeks. . . . I know I really haven't written too much about what happened or what I saw during the war, but I don't really know what to tell you about it. I knew going into it that I was possibly going to have to make some choices that I didn't want to have to make, and see things that I really wouldn't want to see. Well I guess I did, but I'm starting to feel a little better about it. At this point I really just want to get home. . . .

Well considering all goes well I should be there with you at Kelly and Don's wedding. I miss you.

Love,
Jeff

chapter 4
"CAMEL SPIDERS IN MY ROOM"—JEFF IN THE HOME ZONE

WHEN HIS UNIT finally returned from Iraq to Camp Pendleton at the end of the deployment, Jeff was the first to recognize that he wasn't feeling right. He described his war experience on standardized forms he filled out at Camp Pendleton.

BACK IN THE USA

Jeff checked boxes indicating he had seen Iraqi soldiers and civilians wounded, killed, or dead during the deployment; had engaged in direct combat; had fired his weapon; and had felt in danger of being killed. He reported suffering weakness, headaches, numbness, tingling in his hands, light-headedness, diarrhea, and vomiting. Jeff reported that he had put on his gas mask approximately twenty-five times while deployed, had inspected destroyed military vehicles, and had driven by sites that exposed him to fumes, including smoke from oil fires, depleted uranium, and other toxic pollutants. Jeff wrote that he had memories of seeing "dead people." He reported that he had bouts of "little interest or pleasure in doing things" and "feeling down, depressed, or hopeless."

Partway through this screening process, Jeff later told his parents, he was advised by fellow Marines that he should watch what he said unless he wanted to be retained at Camp Pendleton for psychiatric evaluation. His older sister Kelly's wedding was coming up, and he didn't want to risk missing it. So, to the question about having "any thoughts that you would be better off dead or hurting yourself in some way," he said, "No." He also marked "No" in response to "Are you currently interested in receiving help for stress, emotional, alcohol or family problems?"

Jeff was medically and psychologically cleared for demobilization with no referrals for follow-up on July 8, 2003. No one contacted Jeff about the physical symptoms he reported at Camp Pendleton or the impact of his war experiences. There was no debriefing or counseling for family members before or after the Marines returned from Iraq. Jeff arrived back in New Haven on July 13. It was a thrilling moment for Jeff's family and his girlfriend, Julie. Jeff was home safe and sound. Or so it appeared.

After the parking lot celebration that day, they all drove back to the Lucey home. Jeff was excited to distribute some gifts he had bought in Iraq, including scarves and jewelry. He talked about how he overpaid an Iraqi woman for some handmade bracelets. He smiled as he recalled how excited and grateful she seemed to receive five dollars. He shared some other cultural experiences and answered questions until the welcome-home energy started to dissipate.

For Jeff, as for many vets, the long-anticipated excitement of the homecoming quickly faded. Life moves on, and vets and their families try to pick up where they left off, as if a bookmark had been inserted in their home story. But, in fact, the vets and their loved ones have changed during the war, as Jeff had astutely prophesized in his journal. After the reunion, the families drift back to their normal routines, but the vets have to make new ones. The problem is magnified for reservists and National Guard members who demobilize straight back into civilian life without the continuing comradeship available to active-duty personnel.

Jeff got reacquainted with his room. It was just as he had left it. "He was really relieved to be back when he first got home," said his younger sister Debbie. "He looked tired and was thinner, but he seemed fine at first." Yet, increasingly, Jeff's mood began to fluctuate.

Julie had planned a special retreat with Jeff for when he returned. They headed off for a weekend on Cape Cod with a motel reservation near their favorite beach. But Jeff seemed distant. He just wanted to stay in the motel. When Julie suggested a walk on the beach, Jeff responded, "I've seen enough sand to last a lifetime."

Then there was the "Bridezilla incident." Jeff and some fellow Marines came to a buddy's wedding dressed in their formal uniforms. At the reception, they drank heavily, which was a breach of Marine protocol. Nobody would have noticed except that the drunk bride became enraged when the bar closed, threw a tantrum, hurled the cake and gifts around, and fought with police who arrived to restrain her. The scene was recorded on video and ended up on the TV reality show "Bridezilla." It was funny at the time but later an embarrassment for Jeff when they were called out for their misbehavior in uniform.

The next wedding was Kelly's on August 30, 2003. Jeff looked distinguished in his formal Marine Dress Blue uniform, but he stood out. No others were dressed like him. The same uniform that had convinced him to enlist when he saw it on a friend now seemed to set him apart. Jeff had abruptly lost the connection to his fellow Marines when he returned to a civilian family and community life. At one point during the day, Jeff surprised his grandmother by saying, "It's funny that you can be in a room full of people and still feel all alone."

Before the wedding began, Jeff's Aunt Cindy saw him outside alone, staring off into the woods. She approached him and said, "Thank you for going to fight for your country." Jeff glanced at her respectfully and nodded quietly. After a moment, she said, "A penny for your thoughts?" Jeff paused and then responded, "I look out here and it's so calm and peaceful. I can't believe that just a few months ago I was in an area that was totally different. You just don't know what it was like there." It is an age-old paradox that a war veteran's loved ones can never fully understand what war was like.

After the ceremony, Jeff began to drink heavily—again a protocol violation while in uniform. His mother was angry at him and said so. At the reception, there was more alcohol. But, mercifully, no outrageous incidents marred Kelly and Don's big day. Months later, Jeff saw the video from the wedding. "Did I look this bad?" he said. "Yes," his mother replied. "When you drink, everything falls apart."

In the fall, Jeff returned to finish his final year of community college. He took several business courses, earned straight A's, and thought seriously about entering the state police force.

But by the end of the year, Jeff's deeper troubles surfaced.

CHRISTMAS EVE TO SPRING SEMESTER

On December 24, 2003, the Lucey family prepared for its customary Christmas Eve visit to Joyce's parents, who lived a few miles away. The family loved its traditions, and this extended-family gathering had been observed each year since the birth of the first child. On one of the shortest days of the year in rural New England, night came early, and winter's chill had set in. The family gathering, the lights, and the warmth of the celebration offered comfort to offset the cold and darkness.

Jeff had always looked forward to holidays and family rituals. But this time he said he really didn't feel up to going. It seemed odd to his parents, and they asked him what was wrong, but he said it was no big deal and insisted that they go without him. They offered to stay home with him. He said he didn't want them to feel guilty. His sister Debbie, who had always been especially close to Jeff, tried hard to coax him to come. "Don't worry about me, I'll be fine here," he insisted.

So Debbie went to her grandparents' house, but she didn't feel right about it. She left early and headed back home to check on her brother. When she got there, he was in his room. He had been drinking and was in a dark mood. They began to talk and moved into the kitchen. Debbie was upset to see that he had stayed home to drink. She was angry and let him know it.

Jeff silently endured her displeasure at first but then teared up. Suddenly, he blurted out, "Don't you understand? Your brother's a murderer!" He took the two dog tags he carried on a chain around his neck and tossed them at her. Debbie was stunned and confused. For months, she had lived with the regret of a question she wished she could have taken back. Soon after Jeff returned home, Debbie had asked him, "Did you kill anybody?" Jeff had looked her in the eye and then looked away, indicating he had nothing to say. (This blunt question is a mistake many civilians make. Therapists are trained to either wait for the veteran to share that information or open up the subject much more slowly, starting with questions like, "Did you fire your weapon in combat?" or "Did you see anyone fall before you?")

This time, more cautious, Debbie chose not to probe further. After a moment, she side-stepped his self-accusation and said, "No, you're just my big brother." She immediately called her parents, and they came right home. When they returned, Jeff played down the incident. His parents tried to talk with him, but he wouldn't open up, and they spent the rest of the evening at home in silence. Jeff went to his room and didn't reappear until the next morning.

Jeff slept late on Christmas morning, and when he got up his mood seemed much better. He joined the family activities as if nothing had happened. They asked if anything was bothering him, but he didn't reveal anything. Because he seemed to recover so easily his parents wrote off Christmas Eve as just a bad day and a bad drinking episode. However, they began to have nagging thoughts that there could be much more going on than they had thought.

In hindsight, this incident was a turning point. For Debbie, who wasn't living with her parents, this was the first time she really began to notice problems with Jeff. But she never actually told her parents what Jeff had said. She felt at the time that it was Jeff's place to tell them if he chose.

Inconsistently, Jeff revealed bits and pieces of his experiences. However, when questioned directly, Jeff would go outside for a cigarette and return talking about something else. The family was left with a vague sense of the harsh conditions in Iraq and the ugliness of war, but they couldn't draw details out of him directly. Just when he seemed to be opening up, he would maneuver out of the conversation, and the moment would pass. The family shifted back to the only thing they thought would work: comfort rather than confrontation. They offered love, but they weren't trained to take care of a war vet with psychological wounds. What family was?

After the Christmas Eve incident, Jeff's parents pushed him to get professional help, urging him to go to the local Veterans Administration Medical Center (VAMC). He refused because he was worried that seeking help would leave a stain on his record, result in a dishonorable discharge from the Marines, and ruin his chances of becoming a state trooper.

Jeff did attend his unit's post-deployment classes during drill weekends. They included sessions on code of conduct, suicide and drug awareness, Veterans Affairs benefits, and health care. Jeff's fellow Marines said later they did not notice major changes in him after returning from Iraq. Jeff kept quiet, apparently believing that asking for help or even being honest about his experiences would just make things more complicated.

In January 2004, Jeff started spring semester at Holyoke Community College (HCC). He was now majoring in business and was accepted for transfer to the University of Massachusetts in the fall.

Jeff at home, 2003 or 2004.

The veteran agent at HCC hired him to tutor at the career center, a job Jeff enjoyed. Though he got off to a good start academically, Jeff's overall condition worsened over the coming months.

Jeff was increasingly anxious. His combat-ready hypervigilance was evident periodically, like the day when he reflexively dropped to the floor when someone dropped a book in a hallway. He began to have regular nightmares. One night around midnight, Joyce woke to the sound of Jeff screaming, "No!" She called back to him and quickly heard, "I'm OK. I'm alright." Moments later, he yelled, "Fuck!" She went out into the kitchen, and Jeff came in to get some orange juice. He said he was just having a bad dream. He said "they" were coming after him in an alleyway. He tried to describe it, then said he was OK, and went back to bed. Joyce told Kevin but didn't talk with Jeff about it the next day.

Jeff's behavior continued to confuse those around him. Increasingly, he would withdraw into his room. His moods were heavy. Yet these spells were punctuated by moments when he seemed like his old self.

In February, Jeff went with his family and Julie to his uncle's house to watch the New England Patriots play in the Super Bowl. Jeff arrived before the game and talked with his uncle, who had served in the military during Vietnam. When Jeff returned from Iraq, his uncle had given him a knife inscribed, "From a Vietnam veteran to an Iraq veteran." The Patriots won, and Julie and Jeff were ecstatic afterwards. But Jeff's mood turned dark and quiet while driving home with Julie. He interrupted a favorite song, Louis Armstrong's "What a Wonderful World," and declared, "It's *not* a wonderful world."

But Jeff seemed to bounce back from these episodes. On Valentine's Day, he asked his parents if they would leave for the evening so that he could entertain Julie with a special dinner. Jeff liked to cook, and he prepared a delicious lobster dinner that they both enjoyed greatly. Maybe it *could* be a wonderful world?

When *The Passion of the Christ*, Mel Gibson's controversial movie, was released in February, Jeff and Julie rushed off to see it. When they came home, Jeff was adamant that his parents go see it with him that very night. Kevin was puzzled. Though raised Catholic, Jeff had never shown a particularly deep connection with the Church or religion. What was the attraction?

Early in the movie, an apparition tells Jesus, "Do you really believe that one man can bear the full burden of sin?" The movie portrays the savage beatings Jesus endures, and how he refuses to disown his beliefs, submit, or fight back. His mother Mary looks on throughout the ordeal. The movie is hypnotic in its relentless depiction of suffering. Perhaps Jeff connected with its themes of sin, pain, and redemption.

Jeff began to take more interest in his studies. Politics and philosophy suddenly interested him. He described to family members how his philosophy professor would raise important questions and teach the students to think critically. He was learning to think for himself. He began to watch the news regularly and became increasingly opinionated. He spoke more about his reasons for opposition to the war in Iraq. He believed that the war was being fought for the wrong reasons and that the justifications for it kept changing. He was outraged that the country had been duped. When he spoke, his anger at the government simmered just below the surface.

Jeff's drinking increased. Drinking is part of the Marine culture, and Jeff drank periodically when he could in Kuwait. But his relationship to alcohol changed after he returned. Before deployment, he drank socially when he was having a *good time*. Now, he drank because he was having a *bad time*, and things seemed to get worse the more he drank. He used alcohol to cope, to escape feelings, and to numb himself. He drank alone. He hid alcohol and his drinking. He started drinking beer with a higher alcohol content. His favorite became EKU beer from Germany. But he would drink hard alcohol as well, especially Goldschlager schnapps and blackberry brandy. He kept alcohol in his car and sometimes drank between classes at HCC.

His parents tried not to overreact to this at first. They cut him some slack for the difficulty of readjustment. It was a temporary solution, they figured. As time went on and the drinking increased, his parents became more concerned. When they did confront Jeff about it, their focus was on the problems the drinking caused rather than what might be driving his desire to drink. They urged him to at least decrease the drinking and take better care of himself. They talked to him as if he could make that rational choice.

By spring, Jeff admitted that he was using alcohol to escape his pain. When his father brought it up one day, Jeff said, "Dad, I have to. This is the only way I can sleep." Jeff was terrified of his nightmares, so he tried to induce a dreamless sleep by drinking in excess. But the alcohol-induced sleep was not restful, and sleep deprivation became a major concern. His parents became frustrated. He was clearly self-medicating with alcohol yet resisted getting any prescribed medication because he believed that it would be a stain on his record as a sign of weakness and mental instability.

SOCIAL ISOLATION

Of course, Jeff's family dynamics changed as well. The family suffered *secondary trauma* (which I'll explain in more detail in chapter 8) as they tried to cope with Jeff's difficulties. Over time, Kevin felt "sucked into a whirlpool of anxiety, where chaos and emotion became the new normal. Feelings ranged from anger and frustration to fear and utter futility." For his part, Jeff sensed his impact on those around him and began to feel like a burden.

At times, Jeff would sit out on the back deck with a cigarette. His mother sometimes sat and talked with him, but it was as if he were alone, talking to no one, staring off at nothing, his voice a monotone. It was haunting. More than once, Jeff slammed his fist into his other hand, saying, "You just can't understand. You just can't." Then he would apologize for such outbursts.

At school, Jeff began having panic attacks and an exaggerated startle response. It took less and less to make him jumpy. Sometimes it was just a closing door. He felt foolish and awkward and sensed that people were looking at him, though he knew they weren't. In March, he began coming home early from HCC, saying that they didn't need him at the career center or that classes had been canceled. Jeff was slowly withdrawing into another world.

Spring break was a disaster. Jeff and Julie went to Vermont to visit a friend of Julie's. But when they arrived, Jeff was drunk and arguing with Julie. The friend couldn't handle them, and they drove home the next day. A few days later came Jeff's twenty-third birthday and the first anniversary of the war. Debbie threw a party for him at a local pub, but this was a mistake, as his drinking led to more conflict.

After that, with Jeff's increasing seclusion, Julie started to spend a lot of time at the Luceys' house. She stopped arguing with him about the drinking and tried to get through to him in other ways, like encouraging him to go out for walks to talk, but he refused.

Alcohol abuse was linked to Jeff's depression and PTSD, and Jeff's parents now saw it as a symptom. But it clearly took on a problematic life of its own. Trying to control Jeff's drinking became a preoccupation for the family. When one of Jeff's friends brought him alcohol one day, Kevin pounded on the guy's truck and yelled, "You leave him alone! He has enough problems! He doesn't need people hanging around giving him alcohol!" Jeff reacted calmly and said, "Dad, *you* stop it. You're making an ass of yourself." The truth is there wasn't much middle ground between feeling like an enabler and making an ass of oneself.

At the same time, the alcohol sometimes helped reduce Jeff's isolation. He developed a close relationship with the owner of a nearby liquor store, Ye Olde Grog Shoppe. The owner, Ed, had fought in Vietnam. Jeff would stop by after class to buy beer, and the two veterans would sit outside and talk. With Ed, Jeff could open up about his war experiences in a way he couldn't with his own family.

Ed could tell that Jeff was very worried about redeployment. Clearly, he was not ready to go back. At one point, Ed talked to him about whether he had considered moving to Canada. Jeff found that idea fascinating and was curious to learn about Vietnam-era men who had gone that route. But he said he couldn't abandon his unit. Jeff's parents also noticed Jeff's ambivalence about redeploying to Iraq. Jeff would "rant about Bush and what they're doing over there," recalls Joyce, but then he'd say, "OK, I guess I have to go. I hope we go when it's not real hot there." He felt a strong personal allegiance to the other guys. As for many military families during these wars, the prospect of redeployment and the uncertainty about it became a source of constant stress.

Jeff's high school and college friend Shaun said that Jeff didn't drink much before the war, but when he came back from Iraq, his drinking became "disgusting." One day when they took a break to smoke and talk between classes at HCC, Shaun was shocked when Jeff took out a whiskey bottle filled with wine and started drinking. "What's going on, man? What are you doing to yourself?" Shaun asked his friend.[21]

Jeff resisted seeking help, despite his parents' many requests. He was a Marine; he should be able to handle it. He had a T-shirt that said, "Pain is weakness leaving the body." He expressed tremendous fear that if his unit ever found out about what was going on, he would get a "Section 8" discharge (slang based on a World-War-II category for psychiatric illness). Jeff also feared the stigma of seeking help because he believed it would affect his job prospects. These beliefs, an example of what therapists might call *blocking beliefs*, prevented Jeff from getting help and allowed his PTSD to deepen. A blocking belief is a rigid attitude that becomes resistant to change and blocks perceptions to the contrary, thus trapping a person within the belief.

Given Jeff's concerns, Kevin called the nearest VAMC anonymously, explaining that his son was a Marine who had recently returned from Iraq and had been deactivated. He described Jeff's symptoms and issues. The advocate on the other end of the line responded that it sounded like classic PTSD. She reassured Kevin that the Department of Veterans Affairs and the military were separate entities and that legally Jeff's information could not be shared, with his unit or anyone else, without his written permission. When Kevin and Joyce told their son, Jeff seemed open to going to the VA, but with the caveat "when I'm ready, not just now."

Kevin tried his best to be there for Jeff. Sometimes when he returned home from work, often exhausted, Jeff would be waiting for him. "Let's go for a ride. Let's go talk." As in years past, they would drive out to the Quabbin Reservoir, where Kevin had taught Jeff how to drive, or to a nearby town where Jeff had played as a child. Sometimes Kevin even submitted to letting Jeff buy a can of beer to ease the ride. Yet often they drove in silence. Jeff would say that he wanted to talk, but then nothing would come out. At other times, Jeff talked about

Iraq, war, and politics and would often get angry about those topics, but avoided talking much about his own Iraq experiences. When the mood got too heavy, his father got him laughing about memories of his childhood and friends.

Just as he did on the back deck with his mother, Jeff would sometimes stare into space while Kevin drove and talk in a monotone until his voice trailed off. Other times he would sit alone on the deck and cry. Once while they were talking in the kitchen, Joyce said to him, "I just want my boy back," and Jeff reassured her, "I'm right here, Mom. I'm right here."

Those who later said that Jeff must have made up his stories from Iraq as a way of boasting about his exciting war experiences were wrong. He never bragged. His stories came out in fragments, reluctantly, and with self-condemnation for things he had done in Iraq.

There was one place that had offered Jeff a peaceful refuge when he was a child. "The pipeline" was a wooded area that led to a stream where Jeff, his sister, and other neighborhood kids had gone to play or hang out. In the winter, they would sled there. In the summer, a rope swing propelled them into the cool brook. But now that Jeff was an adult, the location took on a new, ominous meaning. Walking there with his sister one day, Jeff pointed to a piece of old rope that still hung from their childhood swing. Although he didn't make any overt statements about his intentions for the rope, Debbie found the experience chilling. She reported this to their parents, and they all agreed to step up their efforts to get Jeff professional help. Later that month, Jeff told Julie about having a rope and tree "picked out" down near the pipeline. But then he said he could never use it because it would hurt his parents. After that, he occasionally alluded to suicide but always followed by saying, "I could never do that because it would hurt Mom and Dad too much."

One day Jeff asked his mother to walk down to the pipeline with him and Shiloh, the family beagle. Jeff gave his mother his earphones so she could listen to a song called "45" by the band Shinedown. It was the same song he had played over and over for Julie and for Debbie and that often reverberated in his room. The lyrics told the story of a young man racked with emotional pain "staring down the barrel of a 45."

Joyce listened to the entire song and then looked at Jeff with concern. Jeff flipped into reassurance mode. "Oh no, Mom, don't be concerned about that. I look at it as a very long tunnel" (in other words, a dark place he would come out of). The mood broke as neighbors passed by walking a llama down to the brook with a picnic lunch, Shiloh barking at the new company. They headed home. Later, Jeff would bring the Shinedown recording to a therapy session and play it for me. (The songwriter has said that it was about trying to "find the strength within yourself to get through" a hard time in life, having to "pull yourself out of a hole," and was "not by any means glorifying suicide." But MTV censored the "45" reference and changed the title to "Staring Down," which led the band to pull it from MTV altogether.)[22]

CAMEL SPIDERS

By this time, Jeff's nights had become an absolute hell. In addition to nightmares, he thought he saw or heard camel spiders in his bedroom. Camel spiders are aggressive desert-dwelling creatures that grow to six inches long, can move at ten miles per hour, make a crunching sound as they walk, and can inflict painful bites, although they are not venomous. They have famously terrified countless American troops in the deserts of Kuwait and Iraq and have inspired the creation of many extreme tales that have circulated on the Internet. While in Iraq, Jeff kept a flashlight handy in his tent for the times he heard the camel spiders crawling around. They disturbed him enough that he often preferred to sleep in the truck rather than the tent.

Back at home, Jeff still kept a flashlight by his bed to be sure he was safe. Creases in his sheets and shadows on the floor began to look unmistakably like large, six-legged creatures. "I'm still freaked out by these spiders," he would tell me. "I have enough trouble sleeping at night, but even when I fall asleep, I wake up half the time thinking I'm being attacked by a spider. I swear I can see them in my room at night." His fear seemed to symbolize much of what haunted Jeff. The camel spiders ignited fear and disgust that likely became linked to other war memories that had followed him home. So Jeff continued to sleep with a flashlight and a knife next to his bed.

Jeff's family was exhausted, pained, confused, and scared. Insomnia, sleep deprivation, irritability, difficulty concentrating, hypervigilance, the exaggerated startle response—all of these things became woven into the Luceys' everyday life. No one knew what to do or where to go except to the VA. Its staff members were assumed to be the experts; they had dealt with soldiers' PTSD for decades. Kevin thought they would be the guardian angels who would hold Jeff in their arms and bring him back to his family.

During this period, Jeff told his mother that he didn't think he was good enough for Julie. It was clear that his behavior was pushing her away. At the same time, he felt that he needed her badly, and he swung between wanting her and trying to let her go. Julie, to her credit, seemed to tolerate a great deal. She encouraged him to go to the VA.

The week before his final exams, Jeff found himself incapable of going to school. He had already been accepted to the University of Massachusetts Business School. One Monday morning in mid-May, however, Jeff told his parents he wasn't going to get up and go to school. He didn't even try to make excuses.

THERAPY

This was the Jeff Lucey who walked into my office in early May 2004—a far cry from the energetic teenager I had seen eight years earlier. Jeff's family was relieved to have him seeing someone. They felt it would take some pressure off of them as Jeff's sole support system.

As a sixteen-year-old, Jeff had been a somewhat brazen kid, but with a likable nature. His behavior had gotten him in trouble like most teenagers, but he was contrite and wanted to clean up his act, though still have fun. I never had to confront him in a harsh manner. I could let him talk through his dilemmas, make a suggestion here or there, and over time help him set goals for himself to stay out of trouble and raise his grades (both of which he did). When our work together concluded, it seemed like he was on the right track.

Now here he was, sitting in the same seat eight years later. In his first session with me, it was immediately clear he had changed. While he was capable at times of being engaged and affable, beneath this veneer I sensed his tension. He couldn't stay in his seat as he once had for an hour at a time. He looked agitated, his eyes darting here and there.

"Do you mind if I smoke?" Jeff asked plaintively. I realized he had been looking for an ashtray or some other signal that he could smoke.

"Well, actually . . ." I started.

As if to save me the pain of saying "no" or perhaps to save himself the pain of having to hear my refusal, he interrupted me. "Do you mind if we go outside?"

This was an unusual request. I'm a psychotherapist. I'm used to sitting with people in an office setting. Sure, I might occasionally go out with adolescents and shoot baskets to build a connection. But with adults, there's an expectation of sitting and finding your way into a conversation. Without hesitation, I realized the answer had to be yes. "Do you want to go for a walk?" I said instantly, half wondering why I had said it. It was a beautiful spring day in New England, the blossoms were out, the air was crisp, and the sun was bright. It was a perfect day for a walk, but what kind of therapy was this? If he went home to tell his desperate parents that he went for a walk with me, what would they think? And yet, I sensed it was what he needed. He could smoke, he could expend some of his nervous energy, and maybe we could connect a bit without the forced awkwardness of sitting face to face.

We headed off for what turned out to be a three-mile walk. Jeff talked nonstop. So much inside of him needed to come out. He jumped right past any caginess about whether he wanted to talk or not. He needed to talk. It wasn't clear where he was headed, but the lid was removed. He wanted me to hear his story. He talked about flashbacks and what we in the clinical world call "intrusive thoughts"—thoughts you don't want to have but can't get out of your head. He had seen his medical doctor and had been on Prozac for five days to treat his depression, as well as Klonopin for anxiety.

He wanted to tell me about the current messiness of his life as he struggled to cope. He told me he was in school but was worried he couldn't finish the semester. He couldn't concentrate and was behind in his work. He was worried about his girlfriend and whether they were going to make it. He couldn't sleep. At times he felt like he was spinning and falling backwards. He said that he hadn't been able to leave his room for about a week.

He jumped quickly from topic to topic. There wasn't room for me to say much, nor did he seem to need me to. In fact, it was clear to me that my role was to keep walking, show that I was listening, and keep from saying something stupid that would shut him down—an important consideration for a civilian therapist listening to a war veteran. That was fine with me. I was relieved that whatever he needed to talk about was coming out, and on his own terms.

Shifting from topic to topic is typical of a first therapy session. When people are upset, their stories usually come out in pieces. Normally, I try to see how the connections of the individual threads of a story reveal underlying issues, even if the big picture takes some time to emerge. In this case, though, the threads ran in every direction. Jeff was clearly overwhelmed. I had many questions I thought might clarify what he was saying, but my first attempt to get more details showed that my questions only distracted him. Jeff clearly wanted to talk, but he responded to my direct questions very selectively. He wanted to be in control of what he revealed. As we walked, we made turns at different roads intuitively without it being clear who had decided to go right or left. At one point, I realized that we were walking in perfect step with each other.

AT THE SECOND session, Jeff came in even more agitated than at the first one. "Can we go for a walk again? I need to get things off my chest," he said. "I need to stop lying to myself."

I took that to mean he wanted to admit what he had been thinking and feeling. And he did. Throughout the walk, he kept repeating, "This feels good. This feels good!"

Jeff talked about Julie, and how despite the usual ups and downs, they had always seemed meant for each other. But now Jeff didn't feel quite as secure in the relationship. He had written his most revealing letters from Iraq to Julie, and she had prayed for his safe return. Nevertheless, Jeff didn't feel like the same person, and he didn't know what that made him to Julie. Amidst his personal struggle to anchor his own psychological experience, to feel OK and safe, he didn't know how to maintain a secure relationship. In his disoriented state, he worried that she was distancing herself from him, which caused his anxiety to rise and his confidence to plummet.

I wondered what it was like to be Julie. What did she see in Jeff when he returned? What did she not see? In some ways he was still her familiar boyfriend, but with his newly wounded and confused soul, he could also seem to be a stranger. Julie had a caring and supportive family, so she had support, but I could only imagine what a strain she was under. Then just as I prepared to ask him a few questions about the relationship, he darted to another subject, and we paced on through this calm, sunny day that was a direct contrast to Jeff's dark and unsettled state of mind.

He told me he'd been drinking more lately. I welcomed that admission as I thought I smelled alcohol on his breath. Should I confront him about it? I was concerned that if I confronted him too bluntly, I could lose his trust, which is a common clinical dilemma. If a client hasn't identified something as a problem, when is it your place as the therapist to point it out? It's generally a risk-benefit balancing act. The potential benefit is successfully bringing a client's awareness to a problem and creating the motivation to change. But the risk is that the client may feel judged or threatened and may drop out of therapy.

Since he had brought the topic up himself, I took a chance. "I have to say, I thought I smelled alcohol on your breath when you first got here." His head snapped back, and he made eye contact with me as we walked. "Wow, I'm surprised you could smell it. I only had a little to drink." I was well aware that "little" is a relative word for people with drinking problems, but he *was* walking normally and talking clearly, so I let it go for the moment.

Then he started in with a series of new stories from Iraq that clearly troubled him. He described seeing an older man, a woman, and a child killed as they tried to flee the streets to a house. "We were told to shoot anything that moves," he added. He told me about the other incident when he took the small American flag from the body of the young boy.

I could tell he was very troubled by these thoughts and desperate to get them out. As our session time was running out, I tried to rein him in to help him get some perspective on his state of mind. I wanted him to realize that he had PTSD and to understand that what he was experiencing was an understandable reaction to what he had been through. I wanted to comfort him by helping him understand that he was not alone, that a description of PTSD and a list of symptoms had been developed because of the many sufferers before him. I said that it was possible to both understand what he had been through and recover from it. I began to talk in relatively abstract terms about how sometimes more help is needed for a person to get back to normal again.

Jeff mentioned that he might be called back for a second deployment in Iraq. He had been told this could occur as soon as June 4, which was less than three weeks away. That seemed astounding to me. Hadn't he been through enough? It was clear that he didn't have it in him to return. I wondered if he could even function there. Just the thought of returning to Iraq was threatening to him. I wondered if there were ways to help him be excused from this redeployment. Jeff said that he didn't want to go, but he couldn't imagine his unit going back without him. He didn't want to let his buddies down. It was a no-win situation.

Then he offered his own solution to the problem. "I've had thoughts of ending it all." This euphemism is familiar to every psychotherapist. Psychotherapists are taught not to overreact or underreact when this issue arises. Any mention of suicide needs to be taken seriously, yet asking questions to learn more and assess the true risk can be a complex process.

I wanted to know how frequently he had considered "ending it all" and what conditions seemed to bring these thoughts to his mind. I wanted to know what feelings came with these thoughts and if any impulses went with them. I wanted to know if he had any specific plans.

I also wanted to know what part of him countered these thoughts and kept him from carrying out a plan. We moved slowly into the topic, but he was not easily forthcoming. As I sought more, he tensed up a bit. It was evident that he had been thinking about this for some time. I asked if he had a specific plan, and he surprised me by saying that there was a tree behind his house down by the stream, and he had imagined hanging from a limb. He said that he had not actually imagined how he would make that happen but just that he had thoughts of hanging there.

There is a general belief in the mental health field that if someone with suicidal thoughts shares them with an appropriate person, it can be a first step toward preventing an actual suicide. That might seem a bit paradoxical, but for people who harbor suicidal thoughts and don't share them, these thoughts can fester. Isolation is fertile territory for disturbing thoughts. So, in a way, I was relieved when Jeff told me about this. Here was a man devastated by what he had been through in the past, gripped by pressures in the present, feeling miserable in his own skin, and looking for solutions.

When working with a patient who has suicidal thoughts, I typically ask, "What is it you wish would end so that you would feel OK?" In most cases, this allows the person to see that it is a problem they want to end, not life itself. From there, we work to address the problem while protecting the life. Somehow I could not get this question through to Jeff in a way that elicited a straight answer. Instead he backed away from the topic altogether.

I persisted with my inquiry and asked if he thought he might follow through with his plan, which he denied. When I respectfully asked why not, he was quick to say, "I wouldn't do that to my parents and family." His response seemed genuine. He had a close-knit family, and his sense of honor and respect were ingrained. His words seemed credible.

I had never lost a client to suicide. I told Jeff that I had talked with many people who felt suicide was their only way out and that I had seen each and every one of them make their way through their hopelessness. I said I was confident that this would be his path as well. Nevertheless, and although he was still trying to distance himself from the discussion, I asked him if he would agree to tell someone close to him if he was having these thoughts.

Despite the normal limits of professional confidentiality, in cases where a client has a high risk of hurting himself or others, psychotherapists have the legal responsibility to take action to protect those at risk, including notifying others. I told Jeff that I needed to be in touch with his parents because I wanted to be able to talk with them about his welfare. I delivered this message as matter-of-factly as I could, but I was still surprised that Jeff did not object. I was relieved that I would be able to consult with Jeff's parents with his consent.

I talked more with Jeff about his drinking. "Maybe you need to be in a program to address the drinking right now," I offered.

He quickly dismissed this. "I can handle what I drink."

I wasn't sure how to respond to this. Mostly, I decided we'd gone far enough for now. I really didn't know how much he'd been drinking or how important it was to him as a crutch. I didn't want to come on too strong, so I moved on.

I told Jeff about a crisis unit he could call and urged him to call 911 if he needed to. I also gave him the phone number of a man named Gordon, who had been in combat as a Marine in Vietnam. Gordon had an engaging personality and conveyed a sense of strength. He was also devoted to assisting other vets and had been working with a local group, the Veterans Education Project. Gordon had spoken publicly about his struggles with PTSD and had sought mental health services in the past from the VA. My hope was that Jeff might call Gordon and find in him someone who could understand his experience thereby encouraging him to seek additional help.

That night I called the Luceys' home and was pleased to reach Jeff's father. I could tell right away that Kevin was relieved to be talking with me. I told him about the community resources available to them. I made sure he had the number of the local crisis unit, and we talked more about the need for what's called in the mental health field "a higher level of care" for Jeff. In my opinion, the ideal would be a residential program that could keep Jeff safe, better assess his needs, and begin to address his PTSD and alcohol-related problems. I told

Kevin that I had given Jeff the name of a Marine veteran, in the hope that Kevin might encourage Jeff to give him a call.

Clearly, we both saw how disturbed Jeff was. We also knew that a big part of the problem was Jeff's unwillingness to get additional help. Kevin and I agreed to stay in touch.

DURING THE THIRD session two days later, Jeff and I took a shorter walk before heading back to my office. Jeff was better able to sit still after the brisk walk and was able to maintain better eye contact with me. First, he talked about school. This was to be his last semester at HCC, but he had frozen up and couldn't complete his work. It would be a disaster if he didn't graduate, he said. I used a problem-solving approach and asked if he could get extensions from his professors. He looked at me and said, "Will you call them?" Normally, I would encourage clients to do something like this for themselves, and coach them through it. But in this case it seemed crucial that he feel somebody's real help. It had taken courage for him to ask me for help, so I agreed.

I called all three of his professors and his advisor the next day. I explained who I was and that I was calling on Jeff's behalf. I said that he was struggling with the aftermath of his military experience and was highly motivated to finish his coursework so that he could move on to the University of Massachusetts. The first professor who answered my call was receptive to this request. She suspected the other professors would be as well. Another one said, "If he's being honest, I'll go to the mat for him." I relayed these responses to Jeff a few days later, and he was relieved.

Despite this problem-solving success, there was still a bigger problem to deal with. As Jeff was leaving the third session, I smelled alcohol on his breath again. Was he drinking to loosen himself up for the sessions, or had this become his daily routine? Either way, I decided to make an issue of it. "Jeff, I can smell alcohol."

"Really?" he replied with a surprised look. "I haven't had much."

"Well, the problem is I don't feel comfortable letting you drive home like this."

"Oh, I'm fine," Jeff said with as much reassurance as he could muster. "I've driven with much more alcohol in me than this."

His honesty was not very reassuring. "I'm concerned about your safety," I said.

"Oh, don't worry, I'll be fine. I'm heading right home."

"You'd probably be OK, but still . . ." I persisted. Then I decided to try a different tactic. "The problem is, Jeff, if anything happens while you are driving, I'm liable because I let you go."

It worked. Jeff's tenor changed immediately. "Oh, OK," he said, and his face now showed concern. He had switched from the struggling, troubled soul to the respectful, do-right-by-people guy who didn't want to disrespect my responsibilities.

"Is there someone who can pick you up?" I asked.

"My parents are at home. I'll call them." He tried but the phone was busy. We talked a bit more and then he called again. The line was still busy.

"You know what? I'm done seeing people for today, and I have to drop something off in Belchertown anyway. I'd be happy to drive you home," I offered. Although this was another therapeutic irregularity, it solved a practical problem, and I hoped it would send a message to him that my concern for his well-being was sincere. I sensed it would strengthen our connection, and it did.

After running my errand, as I got back in the car Jeff turned to me and said, "You see these?" He was holding a thin chain necklace that he had pulled out from under his shirt. At the end of it were two rectangular pieces of metal. "These are dog tags from two Iraqi men," he said. He leaned toward me and gestured that he wanted me to look closely at them. I touched them, turning them over to see both sides, and held them for a moment. I could see writing etched on them, which appeared Arabic to my untrained eye. The tags were metal and light, but their perceived weight felt leaden. The fact that they hung from his neck and rested next to his heart did not escape me. "I killed these men," he explained. "I was ordered to."

Perhaps the environment of the car with no pressure on Jeff to talk made it easier for things to spill out. I didn't want to break the flow. As

I started the car and drove the last few miles, Jeff told me more details. His revelations felt like confessions. Jeff was raised Catholic and had spent time in the confessional. Jeff told me that his hands shook as he pointed his gun at the two men and thought about whether they were sons or fathers. I was riveted by the gravity of his account and knew that it took courage for him to reveal this dark secret.

I didn't feel it was the right time to ask questions or make comments. I sensed that Jeff needed to be in control and that my input would shut him down. Jeff was finally sharing what truly troubled him, but in his own time, and my own desire for details would have to wait.

The Lucey home was just off a country road amidst a grove of pine trees. We parked in the driveway then walked to the door together. Jeff knocked on the storm door, and Shiloh began to bark. Kevin opened the door. Jeff's head was tilted down slightly, and I could tell he expected me to explain what I was doing there.

"I brought Jeff home because I was concerned about his safety when I smelled alcohol on his breath. He tried to call you, but I guess the phone was busy." Kevin thanked me for driving Jeff home. "Jeff's car is still at my office," I said. "You could come back with me now to get it or pick it up any time you'd like."

"Oh, I can get it now, if that's OK," Kevin said.

"That's fine," I said.

Jeff was neither defensive nor apologetic and climbed readily into the back seat. Together, we made the twenty-minute drive back to my office.

I took the opportunity to express my concerns to Kevin about Jeff's safety. Jeff seemed surprisingly comfortable with this, which was a relief, and it opened the gate for further communication between Jeff's parents and me. From that point, there was some sense that we were a team working for Jeff's benefit.

AT OUR FOURTH session, there was positive news. Jeff reported that he had gone to Gordon's house to talk. He was impressed with Gordon, and they spoke for quite a while. He hoped he might land a job with him, as Gordon owned a small business. Gordon also helped him realize that seeking a disability status might actually help him temporarily.

Jeff wanted to walk again. He was still agitated and moved from topic to topic. His father and he had had a long conversation, and he understood that his family was concerned about him.

We mostly talked about the possibility of going to the VA hospital for help. I explained the benefits of being hospitalized for further help and to address his substance abuse. But again, he said he worried about his record.

Jeff's relationship with Julie was still strained. He didn't know how to be a strong boyfriend given how vulnerable he was. He worried about the future of their relationship. And he thought that if he sought help from the VA, it would divert him from school. In his increasingly desperate mindset, delaying meant never graduating. Everything felt like his last chance.

WHEN WE MET for a fifth time, on May 27, the conversation was even more focused than before. It revolved around his safety and his need for more intensive treatment.

More and more, I looked to the VA as the solution—perhaps too much so. They were the experts, I figured. They work with veterans. Many of them are veterans themselves (actually, the majority of the VA staff are not veterans, as I now know). There must be measures in place to protect the interests of service members. They must understand how much resistance a service member has to seeking help.

I was the person Jeff trusted enough to seek help from first, but now I saw myself as the escort to get him to more specialized services. I was quite willing to keep seeing him, to play a role in his recovery, but I knew he needed more. I believed that as long as he was afraid of the military's internal services, the more his inner pressure would be fed.

And now a freight train was coming down the tracks at Jeff: his pending redeployment to Iraq. He was caught in multiple dilemmas. He wasn't prepared to return to Iraq but couldn't let his unit down. He desperately needed more intense psychological help but couldn't face the stigma of accepting it. He relied on alcohol to dull the pain, but his drinking interfered with his ability to seek the help he needed.

Those of us around Jeff were trying our best, but at a fundamental level it struck me that the United States government—from the president to the military to the VA—had sent young people to invade another country without really preparing for the consequences.

chapter 5
"I AM WATCHING OUR SON DIE SLOWLY"—JEFF IN FREE FALL

ON THE FRIDAY afternoon of Memorial Day weekend in 2004, Jeff finally agreed to go to the VA hospital. Joyce, Julie, and Kevin stood tense in the kitchen waiting for Jeff to reluctantly get himself together. They were expecting the bedroom door to creak open but instead heard a thunderous crash from his room. They hustled toward the noise and found Jeff on his bed, gripping his hand. He had punched his bureau, and his fist was all swollen. *Did he think that would stop them from going to the VA? Why was he doing this to himself?* Kevin wondered.

GETTING IN

Jeff's father drove him to the VA medical center, a big, old brick building up a long driveway in Leeds, Massachusetts, about half an hour from their home. Julie rode in back.

I had seen Jeff just five times, starting a month earlier, and knew that he needed more comprehensive help than I alone could provide. His PTSD had possessed him, and in his alcohol-fueled state he was not stable enough to even begin treatment for it. I had recommended that his family check him into the VA to protect and stabilize him. That day, Kevin and Julie had finally coaxed him into the car and even managed to hide the half-full beer he brought along.

65

They parked at the VA building and went in. Kevin explained their concerns about Jeff's safety to the receptionist. He warned her that they had struggled to get Jeff there. When the woman called Jeff over to begin the intake process, Jeff got loud. "What is this, fifty fucking questions?"

A nurse, named Ken Spears, promptly approached them. Ken stood taller than Jeff and had a burly physique. He looked at Jeff squarely and told him, "We aren't going to have any more of that talk. No more shit." Ken revealed that he had been a sergeant in the Marines, and instantly Jeff's attitude slipped away. Everyone felt relieved, as if the whole room had taken a deep breath.

It was three hours after their arrival when the psychologist finally called Jeff's name. The two of them went off to talk, leaving Julie and Kevin in the otherwise empty waiting room. As Kevin sat hoping for a plan to take shape, he prayed to God for help.

When Jeff and the psychologist returned to the waiting room, Jeff displayed a wry, tight smile. The psychologist approached Kevin and Julie. Jeff paced in and out of the discussion. The psychologist told them that the VA programs could help Jeff, and that it would be best for him to stay, but Jeff had declined. The psychologist explained that, contingent upon a doctor's approval, Kevin could push to have Jeff remain under the hospital's care involuntarily. But there was no doctor at the hospital that Friday evening. The hospital would contact the on-call doctor if Kevin and his wife decided to request involuntary commitment.

As Kevin stepped away to call Joyce, Jeff eyed him suspiciously. Kevin hated to think that his son would think of him as the enemy, but he was afraid to return home with Jeff. He had no reason to believe things would get any better.

After Kevin hung up and slipped his cell back into his pocket, Jeff shot to his feet. "We're going," he said.

Kevin looked at his son, wanting to be gentle but knowing he could not yield. He thought about Jeff's bloodied hand and the beer that he had tried to bring along that day. They had been at the hospital five hours now, and, according to the nurses, Jeff's blood-alcohol content was still registering four times the legal driving limit. He didn't even appear drunk, which was alarming. He alternated between looking smug, wild with anger, and now panicked. Kevin knew that underneath every version of his face, his son must simply be terrified. They all were.

Julie pulled her boyfriend into his chair and began feeding him reasons to stay at the hospital and get help. He sat shaking his head "no way" while everyone stood and faced him.

"You only have to stay a little bit longer," offered the psychologist. They were stalling, waiting for the on-call doctor to arrive and sanction Jeff's involuntary commitment.

But Jeff couldn't sit and wait. He got up and walked out, down the steps to the parking lot, and everyone followed him outside. Kevin, Ken, and several other nurses formed a semi-circle around him by the car. Everyone took a stab at getting Jeff to stay at the hospital, but he refused. Just as their efforts began to flag, Jeff announced that he would go back inside on his own volition. Everyone chimed in with, "Yeah, Jeff, that's a good idea." They accompanied him like an entourage back inside, hoping he wouldn't turn and run.

Finally the doctor arrived, in sneakers and shorts. Kevin and Julie went into her office and shared their concerns. They told her about Jeff's references to suicide, his ever-increasing need to drink, his new medication regimen (Prozac for depression and Klonopin for panic attacks), the nightmares, the stories he told, his inability to sleep or to leave the house, his startle responses, hallucinations, deepening depression—a catalogue of painful truths. They described the dog tags Jeff never took off and how he had told his sister Debbie that he had picked out a branch on a tree where he could tie a noose.

After they had given this testimony, Jeff went in to see the doctor. When he came out, he made eye contact with his father and grinned. Then, all at once, he turned and bolted out the front door.

"Jeff just ran out that door!" Kevin shouted.

It took several nurses to wrestle Jeff to the ground once they caught up with him. They handcuffed him and brought him to the locked ward of the hospital. That was Kevin and Julie's last image of Jeff that night. They were told that he had been strapped to a bed and injected with Valium.

One minute, nobody was paying any attention to him as he sat, scared and stirring in the waiting room, and the next, he was shackled and drugged for insubordination. From a trauma point of view, Jeff had spent most of the ordeal in alternating "fight" or "flight" mode. In the end, his attempts to do either were trumped by physical force.

STAYING AT THE VA

That weekend was the first in a long, long time that Joyce and Kevin Lucey slept without the pressure of being on watch. Jeff wasn't hiding in his bedroom stewing, or banging around the house drunk, or sneaking out the window. He was somewhere safe, at least temporarily.

At 6:30 the next morning, Kevin got out of bed and made a cup of coffee. He headed up to the Quabbin Reservoir. He drove the lazy, curved roads letting his mind drift back to better times, like when he had taken Jeff to learn to drive with a coffee in one hand.

That morning, though, he couldn't capture that sense of fun and freedom. It was eclipsed by an ominous weight, a sense of lurking. Kevin felt guilty that he had abandoned his son at the hospital the night before. He turned up the music as he drove home, trying to escape that feeling.

The family visited Jeff at the VA on Saturday, Sunday, and Monday. They brought him clothes and snacks. He seemed to have accepted where he was, but he railed against the regulations imposed upon him. "They said 'smoke time,' and everybody got up to smoke, so I got up too, and they said, 'No, not you.'" Jeff gripped the arms of his chair and shook his head.

Kevin wished that Jeff had signed himself in voluntarily. He told his son, "They wouldn't be watching you so fiercely if there hadn't been a struggle."

Jeff smirked and remarked at how it had taken six people to pin him down the night before. His mom smiled, unsure what else to do.

On their way out of the hospital on Saturday, Kevin and Joyce were told that Jeff could not be evaluated for PTSD until his alcohol issues had been addressed and he was sober. They were advised that when Jeff returned home, if his problems erupted again, they should kick him out so that he would hit rock bottom, or they should call the police and either exaggerate or lie to encourage police action. *Was this the state of the art of PTSD intervention? Was this how the military system cared for its veterans?* they couldn't help thinking. Kevin and Joyce were stunned.

Joyce called me that Saturday before their morning visit with Jeff to inform me that they had gotten him to the VA at last. I checked my messages regularly over the weekend, expecting a call from the VA asking for my input. I had never dealt with the VA before, but it is standard practice for psychiatric hospitals or treatment facilities to contact the patient's primary therapist soon after admission. From this kind of consultation, the hospital acquires relevant clinical history and hears the therapist's concerns about the individual. Likewise, before discharge, the hospital contacts the therapist to inform him or her of the course of treatment and to collaborate in arranging for follow-up care.

I never got a call.

On Monday's visit, the VA staff informed Jeff's parents that there would be a discharge meeting on Tuesday and that they would get a call about it. They assumed they'd be invited to the meeting or involved somehow. So did I. Joyce and Kevin Lucey were capable of understanding Jeff's condition and being an active part of his care. Joyce is a registered nurse and Kevin a social worker who has worked extensively with adolescent and adult criminal offenders.

But the call they received on Tuesday was from Jeff. He said he'd just been released and needed a ride home.

Months later, after considerable effort, the Luceys saw Jeff's records from the VA. His discharge papers stated that he had been treated for "alcohol dependency." They stated clearly that Jeff had reported he was considering killing himself in one of three ways: overdose, suffocation, or hanging.

The VA later justified its lack of communication by saying that Jeff hadn't signed releases to allow a dialogue between the hospital staff and his parents or me. However, they had asked Jeff to sign the releases only on the night he arrived, when he was in no mood to cooperate with anything. I have no doubt that he would have signed a release later in the weekend for them to speak with me.

Joyce and Kevin understood that Jeff's condition threatened his mental, emotional, and physical health. He was "self-medicating" for a reason. He was drinking himself into a corner. He described himself as suicidal, and the only suggestions his parents received were to throw him out of the house if it got to be "too much" or call the police. Kevin had serious reservations about the second option as he had heard about "suicide by police," in which suicidal individuals provoked police officers into shooting them.

Alcohol *was* part of the problem, but it was also part of Jeff's misguided solution to help ease his suffering. Sure, Jeff's drinking needed to be stabilized, and, over this weekend at the VA, this was an important goal. However, the context of Jeff's compulsive drinking—his obvious PTSD—needed to be understood as well.

Although legally an adult, Jeff was still very dependent on his family for help. He had joined the Marines to grow up and to evolve into an adult who could get an education, serve his country, and make a living. But his psychological wounds rendered him a person with more complicated needs. His experiences in Iraq kept him from truly coming back to his rightful place at home. He had regressed, in a sense, back to the helplessness of a child, and he seemed to pine after the air of hope and freedom that had marked his youth.

Joyce called me immediately after Jeff was released from the VA. I offered to see Jeff that afternoon, and when he came in, he was a bit agitated. He seemed happy to see me and eager to talk, but it was hard to tell what he was feeling. It was interesting to hear what he chose to highlight from his VA experience. When he told me the story of how many people it took to wrestle him to the ground, he said it with a hint of swagger, and he was almost smiling. I suppose it was his way of saying that he didn't give in easily to being hospitalized—something he apparently saw as a sign of weakness.

"They watched me like a hawk. They wouldn't even let me shit alone." Jeff thought for a moment and then said, "It's funny. A year ago

I'm walking around with a rifle and grenades. Now they won't trust me with Q-Tips."

As we talked, Jeff's bravado and testiness ebbed, and I could tell that the part of him that knew he needed help was deeply disappointed by the whole experience. When he described being kept in a psych ward with guys who had been there for a very long time, I pictured worn-down Vietnam vets. There was no one his age or who had been in Iraq. Other than a few informal talks with Ken, no counseling was offered, nor guidance of any kind. Jeff told me unguardedly, "I just wanted someone to talk to."

Jeff kept referring to the final interview, which was conducted by a psychiatrist whom he had never met during his stay. She had seemed distracted throughout their twenty-minute talk and interrupted the conversation three different times to answer phone calls. This discharge psychiatrist never consulted directly with the admitting psychiatrist, yet she decided that Jeff was ready to leave the hospital. Jeff told his parents later that he did have something to say to the psychiatrist but never got the chance to.

While part of Jeff felt proud that he had extricated himself from a tight spot, another part of him was perplexed at being dismissed so lightly. When the decision to commit Jeff was made on Friday night, VA staff appeared out of thin air to muscle him into submission, but when he needed someone to make a meaningful connection with him as a veteran and to offer a pathway to recovery, nobody was there.

BACK HOME

Two days after Jeff's release, on June 3, Joyce called Kevin at work. "Be relaxed," she told him. "Stay calm."

That morning Jeff had asked to take the family car for the two-mile drive to get coffee at Dunkin' Donuts. He appeared bright and alert, so his mother gave him permission. An hour later, he appeared at the front door with his head hanging down. He was holding coffees in both hands, but behind him were the Belchertown Police.

While he was driving back home, his car had swerved off the road, jerked up an embankment, and settled between two trees. The officer standing behind Jeff promptly offered that they had checked Jeff for signs of alcohol-induced impairment but found nothing.

The car was totaled. Jeff was in one piece and, evidently, so was the coffee. The incident made me think of the war veterans omitted from the suicide statistics—those who die from single-car accidents, drug overdoses, or violent fights. These are common ways that people end their pain without having to pull the trigger and without the stigma of suicide. On the other hand, maybe Jeff had just run off the road trying to keep two cups of coffee from spilling in his lap.

Saturday, June 5 was graduation day at Holyoke Community College, and both Jeff and his sister Debbie were supposed to graduate. For Jeff, graduation meant an opportunity to continue his studies at the University of Massachusetts in the fall. But Jeff's work was incomplete, so only Debbie would be accepting her diploma. The college invited Jeff to walk with the rest of the graduates in the 11:00 AM ceremony, but he declined. The prospect terrified him. He couldn't deal with the anxiety.

At 9:00 that morning, Jeff popped out of his bedroom. The day was gorgeous and promising. Jeff was unshaven, which was uncharacteristic, but he was chipper and animated. He was excited about the family gathering, and everyone knew how proud he was of his little sister. It was like the old Jeff. They hoped so.

"Hey, Dad," Jeff started. "I'm not ready to leave with you guys. Can I drive myself over later?" Kevin tensed up. Since the accident, Kevin and Joyce had kept all the car keys. But his son's face was earnest and at ease, so he gave the OK.

The whole family, except Jeff, piled out of their cars in the college parking lot. They joined the loved ones of other graduates who were gathered on the lawn, pulsing with enthusiasm. For the time being, it seemed like the Luceys had a modest reprieve from their worries.

But half an hour before the ceremony was to begin, Jeff still hadn't arrived. Then suddenly, there he was. Kevin glared through the mass of people as Jeff was accompanied by a fire department official who reported that Jeff had parked his car over a curb. She had helped Jeff find his parents and said she knew someone in Iraq and understood. Kevin and Joyce headed to the car. Jeff, who they thought was following them, seemed to have evaporated into thin air. Then they saw the bottle of Goldschlager, half-drunk, on the passenger seat. The sight of it was a punch in the gut to Kevin. His hopes for a day of sanity were yanked away, and a surge of anger poured through him. He grabbed the liquor bottle and dumped it in a nearby trashcan.

Jeff's clumsy body emerged from the crowd. There was a grin on his still-unshaven face. Kevin feared a scene and wasn't sure what to say when Jeff insisted that he had to find Debbie to congratulate her. He tore off, weaving through the crowd. He found his sister in a line of students at the foot of the stage. He gave her a hug and congratulated her endlessly. When her name was announced, someone had to tell him to let her go up on stage to receive her diploma.

Once they got back home, Jeff's erratic mood blackened the atmosphere of the graduation party. Jeff's grandmother had never seen her grandson like this. Jeff had always cared about how he looked in front of people and was known for being polite and respectful. His glassy eyes and unkempt hair were like a disguise that the whole family was waiting for him to take off.

Kevin stood in the front yard and called the VA. Nurse Ken Spears was on duty and advised that they get Jeff up there as soon as possible, but Kevin knew the struggle that would ensue if he and his family tried to cajole Jeff into going. He hung up and took a deep breath. He didn't want to call the police so he dialed the local twenty-four-hour Emergency Services unit for mental health crisis intervention. Emergency Services staff members are contracted by the state to provide assessment and emergency intervention and to determine if an involuntary inpatient stay is necessary. Kevin explained the situation, and the crisis worker asked a series of questions. When she asked if Jeff had been drinking, the inquiries abruptly stopped. "Well, then, we can't help," she told Kevin.

It didn't matter that Kevin had already told this person that his son had mentioned suicide. It didn't matter that he had recently been committed at the VA hospital. It didn't matter that they, his family, had lost all hope of handling the situation alone and were in need of aid.

We can't help.

Kevin heard voices carrying on in the backyard and clenched up at the thought of what Jeff was undoubtedly doing and saying.

"You'll have to call the police," continued the voice on the phone.

He wanted to scream at the top of his lungs, *You are setting people up to die!* But he hung up the phone instead. He pictured cops arriving at their house. He imagined Jeff's face changing when he saw them, knowing why they were there. In other drunken fits over the past few weeks, his son had spewed out warnings that if the police were called in, someone was going to get hurt. Kevin thought again of police-assisted suicide. No, the only way to get Jeff back to the hospital was to play the game again. They had to reason with him; they had to convince him.

Kevin returned to the party. Joyce was pacing. Jeff was asking his grandma if he could use her car. He pleaded, "I haven't gotten Debbie a graduation present yet," but Grandma didn't fall for it. Debbie was on the front steps crying.

Jeff wanted his sister Debbie to play whiffle ball with him. He kept asking her to play. "Like when we were kids," he said. He was becoming incoherent. Finally, Debbie got him to agree that if she hit ten of his pitches, he would go to the hospital.

Jeff could barely stand, let alone pitch. He stumbled around their makeshift pitcher's mound and fell down.

Finally, when Debbie hit the ball for a third time, she lied, "Come on, Jeff, that was ten." He was too impaired to know the difference and believed her. Defeated, he hung his head and began to walk inside. He didn't fight—this agreement was one he would honor.

Jeff wouldn't let his father come along, so his brother-in-law, Don, drove, with Grandpa riding shotgun. Jeff sat in the back seat between his two sisters. He joked about how they always rode that way when they were kids. They left the party and headed for the VA again. Debbie can't remember if they ever even served the cake. "I think we threw it away," she said later.

LOOKING FOR HELP

When they arrived, Jeff wouldn't go up to the building. Several nurses and guards stood outside the hospital with Jeff's crying sisters and pleading grandfather.

Jeff couldn't even walk. His feet were crisscrossing in front of him. He wasn't asking to leave, he wasn't fighting it, but he didn't go into the building either.

"We can't take him back," Kelly said to her grandpa.

Her grandpa turned to the hospital staff. "You have to take him."

But they wouldn't. They said that he wasn't admitting himself voluntarily, and there wasn't a doctor present to authorize an involuntary commitment. Nobody suggested that they call a doctor to come in like the last time. Kevin wasn't there to ask. Jeff had been there less than a week before. They knew about his drinking, his car wreck, and his talk of suicide. He was obviously just as bad, or worse, and the family was desperate.

Debbie believed that Jeff was waiting for the hospital staff to tell him that he didn't have a choice. "He wouldn't have sat there cooperatively if he didn't know that he needed help," she later said. "Jeffrey just wanted to feel normal, and didn't want to ask for help. When the staff left us out there on the lawn, Jeff looked sad."

Perhaps he felt like everyone was giving up on him anyway, like he wasn't worth their time.

Debbie phoned her parents to say that they still had Jeff and that they were coming back home with him. Joyce and Kevin were stunned. They realized it was all on their shoulders to keep him safe. They wracked their minds to imagine how he might hurt himself at home that night. They scurried around the house hiding anything they thought he might use. They found alcohol stashed and threw it out. They cleared the kitchen of all knives except butter knives. They disabled his car by yanking out the fuses. They hid dog leashes.

Kevin called me and explained what had happened at the VA. I was discouraged. I had banked on the notion that the VA was the most appropriate place to serve a wounded veteran. I assumed that VA staff members were the experts on reaching out to veterans, and if they couldn't justify a mandatory commitment with all the evidence that had been provided, then they must have assessed Jeff as a low safety risk who did not require intensive treatment. I certainly wanted to believe that, though I knew his resistance to seeking help was a factor.

It wasn't clear what to do. I felt the added pressure to work even more closely with the family and do what I could to help stabilize Jeff in our sessions. But the burden of witnessing Jeff's day-to-day activities fell upon his parents.

When I next saw Jeff a few days later, he seemed to be doing a bit better. He reported that he had not been drinking much lately, although he admitted that he had been smoking a lot of pot. He found that it was more effective at making him feel calm, and for now this seemed the lesser of two evils. He remained worried about his relationship with Julie and how long she would stick with him in such a broken-down state. I said that I suspected Julie cared very much about him and that she probably believed he could get better and return to his old self. I tried to help him believe he could recover one step at a time. He could still barely see a day in front of him, but I tried to reassure him with specific examples of how these steps could lead to a fulfilling future.

We discussed his suicidal thoughts. I told him that I had known many people who were suicidal and how, in the midst of their misery, they could never see that those feelings would change. Yet, six months or a year later, they found themselves feeling better and grateful that they were alive. When I shared this with him, I assumed he understood because his body would relax. He reassured me again that he would never take his own life because of the effect it would have on his family.

I thought that he was gaining some perspective that even though he was depressed and had PTSD, the condition would not be permanent. He seemed to be adopting a more practical approach, and he considered filing a disability claim for more financial security while he restored his health. Unfortunately, as his family and I soon discovered, Jeff could not sustain these more sensible moments.

A few nights later, Jeff dressed up in full military uniform and climbed out his window. He and his parents had just finished watching the Red Sox game, and he had retired to his room. Joyce and Kevin assumed he was resting for the night.

Debbie called home and asked if they knew where Jeff was.

"He's in his room," said Kevin. "Why?"

"You'd better check," she told her dad.

Debbie had received a call from their neighbor. She told Debbie, "I have your brother in my car. He wants me to take him to get alcohol down the street."

Debbie instructed her to drive slowly back to the Luceys'.

Kevin ran out to the driveway as the neighbor pulled up with Jeff in the back seat. Jeff climbed out of the car in his Marine "cammies" with two KA-BARs—seven-inch Marine Corps combat knives—and a six-pack of beer. He looked to his parents like a soldier coming out of the bush in Vietnam. He was wearing the green uniform appropriate to rural Massachusetts, not the desert-colored camouflage he wore in Iraq. He was on a mission. In his belt holster, he had a pellet gun that he'd managed to hide from his parents.

Kevin thanked the neighbor for bringing Jeff home. He snatched the beer from Jeff and started hurling one bottle at a time at a nearby tree. Jeff stood there, frozen stiff, until his mother hurried out and took the rest of the beer. She walked inside with her son following behind her asking, "Mom, can I just have one beer so I can go to sleep? Mom?"

The family was now continually braced for the next incident with Jeff. Joyce still wished she could fill him with hugs, with affection, and let the warmth of their family bond melt all of his hurt away. But she knew it wasn't so simple.

After Kevin's outburst, his anger subsided. It was replaced with despair. He half-wished that an eighteen-wheeler would veer into him on the highway. It wasn't a suicidal impulse but a feeling of despair. He felt alone and thought no one cared, just as Jeff did. The family was living full-time in Jeff's hell.

One night soon after, Jeff approached his father, who was sitting at the computer. "I need to talk," Jeff said. He had a bottle of beer in his hand. Kevin asked him to wait a minute while he finished his paperwork and started printing his documents.

But Jeff couldn't wait. He started going off about the war. He ranted on and on, and when he noticed he didn't have his dad's full attention, he slammed his beer on the desk, spraying it onto the printer and the wall. Before Kevin could even react, Jeff turned on himself. He lifted the bottle back up and started to inch backward, as if trying to rewind his angry outburst, but tripped and lost his balance, landing between a chair and an end table. The rest of his beer splattered against the wall.

For a moment Jeff just lay there, half-propped up against the furniture, shaking his head back and forth. He said he was sorry for being "such a fuck-up."

The next Monday, June 14, Kevin came home from work to find Jeff sprawled in front of the fireplace smoking. He had surrounded himself with open books on PTSD, which his father had ordered.[23] Kevin sat down on the couch, and Joyce leaned on the doorway to the living room. They listened while their son went down the list of symptoms.

"I've got this one," he said. "And I definitely have that one." Jeff continued until he had realized, out loud, that he had nearly every symptom on the list. Kevin and Joyce watched their son look up with tears in his eyes. "I feel like I'm going crazy," he choked out.

Kevin cleared his throat. As if trying not to startle a deer that had crept onto their front lawn, he spoke gently. "Are you willing to get help?"

"Yes."

THE VET CENTER

The next day, Joyce called the VA again. She dialed the same number of the same place they felt had failed them the week before and the week before that. What new way could she convince the people on the other end of the line that they were desperate?

"I am watching our son die slowly," she told them. "We need help, and we need it now!"

This time there was a new response. For the first time, someone from the VA mentioned the Vet Center to the Luceys. It was a place in Springfield, Massachusetts, about an hour away, that catered to vets and their families. Why hadn't the VA mentioned this before?

It was obvious upon making contact with the Vet Center that they were immensely better equipped to deal with Jeff's circumstances than the VA hospital had been. Congress established these centers in 1979 after Vietnam to meet the needs of veterans by providing a more community-based, less bureaucratic, and more user-friendly branch of the VA medical system. They offered services never mentioned at the VA. I was pleased to learn of the Vet Center and what it had to offer Jeff. But I was upset with myself that I had not known of it or done more ground work to look for resources beyond the VA. Later I learned that none of my community-based colleagues knew of it either.

The Vet Center scheduled an appointment for Jeff three days later. For the Lucey family, hope was renewed. Jeff had apparently stopped drinking that week while they anticipated the prospect of a fresh chance at help.

Jeff and his father went to the appointment together and met with a social worker named Jaime Perez, a Marine who had served one tour in Iraq as a mental health specialist and would go on to serve multiple redeployments. Jeff and Jaime seemed to get along well, and the three of them talked for two hours about options. Jaime spoke of a couple of different residential programs that were equipped to address both Jeff's PTSD and his substance abuse problems. Together, they decided that inpatient treatment was the best idea. They formed a plan. In addition to his sessions with me, Jeff would see Jaime regularly until Jaime could locate a bed for Jeff at an appropriate facility.

CAMP SUNSHINE AND BACK

The next morning was Saturday, and the Luceys headed off in two cars for a much-needed retreat to Casco, Maine, where the family had long made yearly summer visits. They headed to Camp Sunshine, the retreat for children with cancer where Jeff and his sisters had volunteered to help lift the spirits of the families. Kevin hoped that it would give all of them a new perspective on life and, in turn, lift his son's spirits as well.

The first night was a staff-only, twentieth-anniversary celebration banquet. As the Lucey family members were settling into their rooms and making their way to the event, Jeff had already discovered the bar. He soon caused a ruckus, and the camp officials asked him to leave. The weekend that had seemed so promising was now another door slamming in their faces.

At 10:00 PM, Kevin left the party with Jeff for the four-hour trip home. Joyce and Debbie decided to leave in the second car even though they had originally planned to stay several days longer. But they couldn't find their car keys. They ripped through their suitcases and handbags but came up empty. Kevin and Jeff were out of cell-phone range. On a Saturday night in the Maine woods, one couldn't call a locksmith, so Joyce and Debbie had no choice but to stay.

Kevin and Jeff arrived back in Belchertown at 2:00 AM on Father's Day morning. Kevin told me later that it had been a long ride during which he had tried to talk to his son, but after a few minutes Jeff pretended to conk out. Then he would straighten up and stare out the windshield or, every so often, change the radio station. Just before they got home, he fell into a restless sleep, so Kevin left him in the car and watched from the living room window until he got up and came in around 4:00 AM.

Jeff stayed in his room most of the following Sunday. He wished his dad a happy Father's Day and kept trying to apologize. He felt guilty for not getting him a gift. "The only gift I want," Kevin told him, "is for you to be able to handle your PTSD and feel happy again." Joyce, still stranded in Maine, called home throughout the day for updates.

Later that evening, Jeff wanted to talk. He felt helpless, he told his dad. Kevin reminded him of how he had gone through the books on PTSD and identified his symptoms. Wherever there were symptoms, Kevin said, there would be solutions. They discussed his drinking. They discussed Jeff's fear that he had lost his girlfriend. Jeff kept repeating that Julie deserved better. The conversation swung to Iraq, to the guys in his unit, to his desire to have more family gatherings, and then back to Julie. Jeff desperately tried to make sense of his turmoil. Kevin tried to get him to focus on the present and, more importantly, on the future.

"You could turn all the negative into positive," Kevin said, in his most encouraging voice. He wanted so badly for his son to see this. "You could help others who are going through the same stuff as you are."

Jeff knew how much stress he was putting on the family, and he told his dad as much.

"Right now," Kevin said, "you are going through a tough time. But others before you, throughout the centuries, have been able to turn it around, Jeff. And survive. And manage the PTSD." To Kevin, it felt like a good conversation. He had reminded Jeff that he had always been one to help others when he was growing up and that now it was time to help himself. He went to bed that night hoping that these thoughts would linger with Jeff and inspire the tenacious side he knew he had. Kevin lay in bed and thought about the end of the conversation. His son had told him that he was proud of him. Kevin, of course, told Jeff how proud he was of him, too. He said, "You know, you can have a tremendous life, Jeff. You can overcome this." They hugged. They both had tears in their eyes.

Jeff came to my office on Monday. His grandfather brought him, because his mom and sister were still in Maine, and Kevin was at work. Jeff reported that on the way, his grandfather had taken the opportunity to stop by a cemetery not far from my office where his own parents, along with two uncles and an aunt, were buried. (As I later learned, one of these uncles had died from a self-inflicted gunshot in the 1930s.)

When I saw him, Jeff told me about what had happened at Camp Sunshine and how much he had upset his family. He was clearly embarrassed but not overly emotional about it. I talked with him about the importance of being able to forgive himself. I tried to be at once compassionate, forceful, and hopeful.

He told me about his meeting with Jaime at the Vet Center. He felt comfortable with Jaime, and, overall, he seemed calm. This seemed like a very good sign. At the time, I thought perhaps he was accepting himself. But in retrospect, perhaps he was coming to another decision.

That night at home, Kevin saw a different Jeff than the one I had observed earlier. He was edgy. They got into another deep discussion, though Jeff kept going into his room momentarily and then popping back out. Kevin believed he was trying to contact someone by phone. Maybe Julie.

As the night wore on, the conversation between father and son became more and more bleak. Jeff was enraged. He hated the president. He hated the government. His jaw was clenched, and he was spraying spit as he yelled. He said that he could hurt himself; that he could kill himself. He took his father downstairs to the basement. He pointed and said, "I could put a rope around this pole and this pole."

Kevin went upstairs in a state of panic. He called the Vet Center and managed to get in touch with an on-call staff member. He put Jeff on the phone and left them to talk, hoping it would stabilize things for the night. The plan was for Jaime and the rest of the team at the center to meet the following morning to hammer out a more structured plan for Jeff until they got him into residential care. But Jeff told the staff person on the phone that "no one cares enough to help."

That's how Jeff felt, and his father didn't know what else he could do. Such was Jeff's turmoil. At one moment, Jeff didn't want help but then was desperate for it. He didn't trust others who showed concern but then felt no one cared. He was doing fine but then was despondent. His father seemed to have reached him, but then Jeff seemed far away. All these features reflected a fragmented inner condition.

Eventually, Jeff calmed down. For dinner, Kevin cooked up some steaks. Jeff normally loved steak but this time said, "No, I'm not that hungry."

At around midnight, Jeff crept into the living room where Kevin was sitting in his armchair. Jeff asked if he could sit in his father's lap. To Kevin, it harkened back to days when Jeff used to crawl into his dad's lap for comfort as a child. It wasn't the first time he had requested this. A few weeks prior, Kevin and Jeff had been in the living room, along with Debbie and her boyfriend. When Jeff came over to his father and asked the same question, the room had cleared out. Soon it was just a father soothing a son.

Kevin sat there, stroking his son's head.

Before Jeff went to bed, Kevin suggested that they go to a favorite steakhouse the following evening. Kevin remembers making some stupid joke, and that they laughed, and Jeff went off to bed.

END OF THE ROAD

Kevin went to work Tuesday morning and called during the day to check in with Jeff. Jeff didn't pick up, but this was not unusual.

Jaime Perez called me that afternoon. We talked for half an hour. While he didn't review with me the events of the night before, he asked if I thought Jeff was suicidal. I said that I had been concerned about that for quite a while. Jaime explained that they had identified two inpatient facilities that might be appropriate for Jeff. One treated substance abuse for thirty days, then focused on PTSD for thirty days, and had a bed available. The other employed a treatment model that simultaneously addressed PTSD and substance abuse. While this seemed like the best model for Jeff, they did not have a bed available. I said, "Take the bed."

Jaime told me that he planned to drive out to Jeff's house at the end of the day. As it turned out, Jaime left a message for me that evening saying he had gotten lost on the country roads and was heading home. He'd call Jeff the next day.

At about 5:00 PM, Kevin headed home from work. As he drove, he realized how raw and tired he was—from the last two nights of intense discussion with his son, and from his fear. He didn't know which Jeff he would be dealing with when he arrived, and he was feeling sorry for himself. All he wanted was to pick up his son, go down to the steakhouse for a nice dinner, and then get home to watch the Red Sox together.

Still in Maine, Joyce called Kevin on his cell phone when he was almost home. In fact, they were on the phone when he pulled into the driveway. Kevin could see the glow of the TV through the front window and remarked to her that their son was, no doubt, lying in front of the fireplace, smoking.

"I'm going inside," he told his wife, "I'll call you back later." Kevin gathered up his newspaper and briefcase and went inside. Shiloh, their beagle, greeted him. He thought about the times when the kids were young that he would come home to find his living room furniture transformed into a fortress, with unabashed giggles leaking out from behind the couches and chairs. Jeff and his sisters would be clutching their dog Starsky's collar, holding him back as he tried to sneak out and meet Kevin as he walked through the door. Sometimes Joyce would be huddled in the fort, too, holding back laughter.

Jeff wasn't in the living room, so Kevin called out for him and walked through the kitchen and down the hallway to his room. Jeff's bed was made. On top were the dog tags that he had worn every day since he returned from Iraq.

Kevin figured that some friend of Jeff's had come to pick him up to take him for a ride or a walk. Or maybe to the liquor store. As Kevin headed back to his car to bring in more paperwork, he noticed the basement door was open and the light was on. He could vaguely make out the shape of a few framed pictures on the cellar floor. Confused, he went down the stairs. He was focused on the photos that had caught his eye. As he got closer, he noticed what seemed to be handwritten letters strewn on the floor. The letters appeared to be stained red. The framed pictures were family photos and pictures of Jeff's Marine buddies. They were arranged in a semi-circle with pictures of his sisters, his parents, and Jeff's platoon photograph in the center.

Kevin was confused. As he stood there staring, he caught a glimpse of something in the corner of his eye and turned his head. For a moment, it looked like Jeff was standing there with his eyes peacefully closed. Then Kevin saw the hose.

Howling, Kevin ran to Jeff. He buttressed him up on his knee, held tightly to his son's chest, and lifted him so that he could get the hose from around his neck. Jeff was cold, and the chilled dampness of his body went right through Kevin's clothes to his skin.

He sat with his son in his lap for the last time.

THE AFTERMATH

At first Kevin was light-headed, trying to breathe, watching the scene as though outside his own body. His efforts at resuscitation were hopeless, and he ran upstairs and called 911. He went back down and held Jeff's blood-stained hand in his own. He heard a dog barking, far, far away. It was Shiloh, upstairs, barking at the Belchertown police. Kevin knew the officers. They came down and tried CPR. "Don't waste your time," Kevin said. "He's gone." The state police arrived and interrogated Kevin like a suspect.

The phone rang. Kevin looked at the caller ID and didn't want to answer. He picked up the phone but couldn't speak. Joyce asked, "What's wrong?" Kevin choked. Joyce's voice cracked, "Is it Jeff? Is he OK?" Hearing no answer, she probed, "Is he dead?"

Kevin could only manage the words, "Something has happened to Jeff."

Debbie was standing next to her mother yelling, "Why isn't he answering?" They were both dressed in animal costumes for the Camp Sunshine evening festivities. It was surreal.

Kevin said that he was headed to the hospital, and that he'd have to call back. His brother arrived and drove him there. En route, Kevin called Kelly, and her husband, Don, answered the phone. Kevin came a step closer to saying Jeff was dead. Meanwhile, Debbie called Kelly and said she thought Jeff was dead.

When Kevin reached the hospital, Kelly was outside, sobbing. She had tried to see her brother, but the hospital staff had escorted her to the chapel and told her that he was dead. She bolted outside. Don chased her but she wouldn't let him or Kevin come near her.

Debbie and Joyce tried to weave their way out of the crowded activity cabin. Music was playing, and everyone else was laughing. Debbie could see mouths moving but could hear nothing but a blur. She told a staff person that she thought her brother was dead. They ran through pouring rain and lightning to the office building, peeled off their costumes, and tried to call Kevin, without success. Joyce sat against the wall with her knees up saying, "He's dead. I know he's dead." They still had no vehicle because of the lost keys, but the camp staff went into action to get them back home. People threw their belongings into trash bags to get on the road, and Joyce and Debbie drove off in the back seat of someone's car, as Debbie screamed that it was all her fault, and she didn't get a chance to say goodbye to Jeff. She was close to vomiting. Then there was mostly silence on their five-hour drive.

That evening, something compelled me to check my office messages. Minutes earlier a call had come in from Debbie. As soon as

I heard her voice, I feared the worst. "Something happened to Jeff. I think he's dead. My father's at the hospital. My mother and I are driving home from Maine right now. I don't know what the cell phone coverage is going to be like." I tried to reach Debbie but couldn't. I called local hospitals. I knew that they couldn't legally tell me the name or condition of a patient, so I asked for Kevin Lucey. I finally found the right hospital, but they said he was unavailable.

Debbie called Julie, whose mother answered the phone. "Jeff died," she blurted out. Julie's mother handed the phone to Julie. Debbie repeated, "Jeff's dead," and Julie began screaming. Her mother drove her to the hospital.

Kevin, Kelly, and Don headed back to the house. Don helped Kevin clean up the broken picture frames, separating the photos from the blood-stained, broken glass. The organ harvester called around midnight to arrange for Jeff's organs to be donated.

I reached Kevin later that night, and he told me what had happened. I offered to come over, but he wanted to be alone. I was worried about him but respected his choice. He went to Jeff's bedroom and sat on his bed. Then, exhausted, he collapsed in the chair where he had rocked his son the night before. His mind was whirling, his heart empty. He dreaded the return of the rest of his family.

When they arrived, around 1:30 AM, Kevin switched gears and changed his focus. He told himself, "I better take care of the living."

chapter 6
GOING PUBLIC—FIGHTING STIGMA AND SPEAKING OUT

FOR JEFF LUCEY, June 22 was an end. Frozen in the finality of the moment, the Luceys could never have predicted that they were about to begin a new journey. Step by step, they faced their loss and began a decade-long campaign to bring attention to the needs of veterans and their families, to push the government to do better, and to help our society overcome the deep stigmas around mental health and suicide.

THE MORNING AFTER

The morning after Jeff's death, I called the house, and Joyce picked up. She was overwhelmed but still able to talk. Amidst everything, she was suddenly aware that there was now a public component of this ordeal, starting with the preparation of a funeral.

Indeed, the news about Jeff's death went through their small town quickly. Up until then, it seemed the wider world had not paid enough attention to Jeff, but now suddenly all eyes were on the situation.

This was a pivotal point. Joyce became aware that this would not simply be a private family matter. On the phone, I tried to help her realize what had happened to her family would affect many others. It would be understandable, in the aftermath of this tragedy, for the family members to blame themselves or Jeff. But, especially given the exhaustive efforts the Luceys had made to seek help for Jeff, it seemed important to share the responsibility broadly and see it in a larger context of war and its consequences on society. It was clear immediately that the Luceys would forgo their own privacy and refuse to bear the responsibility for this loss alone. Although quite unusual for loved ones after a suicide, they chose a path of sharing their story openly. They believed that the only solace they could conceivably take from Jeff's death was the prospect that others would not suffer a similar fate.

But it wasn't an easy path to choose. They had no idea how others would view their experience. They wondered if anyone would care or, worse, would they receive harsh judgment that would compound their pain? Would people see Jeff's death as a marker of a broader systemic problem or merely view the Luceys as angry, ineffective parents of a defective child, who wanted to place the blame elsewhere? Would they recover at all? Many times after the death of a young child or even an adult child, the marriage doesn't survive. Would speaking out be a pathway to healing, or would their guilt, anger, and grief interfere with their goal of bringing needed light to a dark topic? They were a family in turmoil.

Kevin and Joyce had not been public people. They, especially Joyce, had never been political in any visible way. But they had formed increasingly strong views about the government's responsibility for a war that they believed was started by a deceptive and manipulative president with a hidden agenda. Up until this point, they had never written or spoken about it. As Kevin would say later about opposing the war, "We didn't really go into that direction. We stumbled into it." Joyce added, "At that point I was very angry about the war."

What I remember most from that conversation with Joyce was that there was some sense of resiliency, of pushing back. She was devastated and disoriented, but she was also angry—angry that it had come to this. Through a haze of shock, grief, and guilt, she told me of her determination to "keep this from happening to the other Jeffs of the world."

MY REACTION

I was in my own kind of shock. That evening, I drove by the house of a colleague and friend who lives nearby. He happened to be outside in his garden, so I pulled over. After talking about his garden for a while,

I came out with it: "A client of mine committed suicide yesterday." Fortunately, he was able to sit down and talk. I needed to begin my own process of reevaluation and recovery.

Never before had a client of mine taken his or her own life while working with me. As mentioned, I had helped many people get through such a crisis and later appreciate how much better they were doing. Clients had expressed relief and astonishment to me when they no longer had suicidal thoughts. These recoveries buoyed my faith in the resilience of the human spirit. Over time, the authority with which I could offer hope to new clients grew stronger, and, in turn, they expressed that my confidence helped them believe in themselves. Now, that faith was shaken.

With all my years of experience, suddenly I felt naïve and inadequate. I thought I had been aware of the real risks for Jeff and had worked hard within the limits of my professional capacity as a private therapist. Still, I wondered if I had misjudged the problem. In hindsight, I was learning about a higher level of risk that can exist for veterans in the aftermath of war.

I know that it is common to also feel anger at a person who takes his or her own life. Doesn't that person understand the impact their action has on others? Doesn't he or she understand that people will never forget? To the loved ones, suicide can seem like a selfish act. Lives are intertwined, and when one person exits, he or she takes away a part of the survivors' lives as well. And this impact can last sometimes for generations. Yet those who take their own lives generally don't understand this, at least not at that fatal moment, and that's a big part of the problem. Could Jeff have prevented this? In a healthier state of mind, of course, but under these conditions, evidently not. I'm sure he frustrated a lot of people who tried to help him. But I didn't feel blame toward him. I felt compassion. I still saw him as that teenager with so much to live for, not as the lost and tormented soul he had become. A person's descent to the bottom is often ugly and can leave many hurt and resentful. But I do not believe that anyone would take that route if he or she truly understood there were other options.

I had expected Jeff would get through this bad phase. I had envisioned that someday, when he was more stable and ready, I would be able to help him face those disturbing experiences from Iraq and come to terms with them. I had even anticipated that in a year or so when he was back on track, he and I would share the satisfaction that his life was OK. Now that possibility had passed.

My mind turned over every detail of my involvement as I reviewed reason after reason for why this might have happened and what might have prevented it. I wondered what I *could* have done differently but, more hauntingly, what I *should* have done differently. Had I failed in my capacity? I believed that the Lucey family had done all that they could do, but their determination was not enough. I had expected much better service from the VA and the local crisis response systems, but my criticisms offered little relief. I regretted that I had relied so much on these services and that I had not known of the Vet Centers and other resources beyond the VA. I wished that I had met with Jeff more often. Suddenly, I wondered if every extra step I could have taken might have been enough to change this outcome.

Eventually, and it took quite a while, I had to settle with the belief that I had done what I could or at least what I thought I should. Apart from grieving this tragedy and the loss of Jeff, I saw no value in hanging my head. Yet I could not simply seal this experience away, nor did I want to. I wanted to learn from it, though I had to accept that new knowledge could not change the past. Yet, because I would never know exactly what went wrong for Jeff, it didn't mean that I should stop asking questions about it. And what I've learned, including what is reflected in this book, has made me wiser and has guided me as I move forward.

To my relief, the Luceys did not then, nor ever, express dissatisfaction with my involvement. This made it easier to follow my inclinations and support them as they dealt with this tragedy. It's a decision that has influenced my life and work for the last ten years. The Luceys never became professional therapy clients, but I remained connected with them and their subsequent journey. In my own way, I allied myself with them to create change, including speaking together in public presentations and trainings later on.

But that future was far from anyone's mind the day after Jeff died.

That morning I called Jaime Perez from the Vet Center to tell him what had happened. He, too, was shaken. He wondered if he would have found Jeff alive had he arrived as planned instead of getting lost. We pieced together the events and realized that Jaime, who had left his office at 5:00 PM, would have arrived about an hour after Jeff's death. Jaime would have arrived before Kevin, however, and perhaps this was in Jeff's mind. Jaime and I expressed our shared remorse that we weren't able to get Jeff into a residential facility.

THE WAKE AND FUNERAL

The wake and funeral brought together hundreds of friends, loved ones, and others from the community. I arrived at the wake to see a line going out the door of the funeral home. I was full of emotion but felt my role was to try to remain professional and attentive to others. My therapy practice had started in Belchertown, and there were at least a dozen people at the wake whom I had seen as clients at one time or another. I felt more like my father, the minister, than a psychotherapist. All I could offer was an understanding gaze and handshake to those who knew me. Their faces in turn revealed shock, confusion, and sorrow.

The wake itself was a moving event. Julie, Debbie, and Kelly had created a video slideshow accompanied by Jeff's favorite music. His spirit came back to life as the images flashed on the screen. The funeral director was moved to tears. Members of Jeff's Marine unit arrived in dress uniform, as well as Jaime and the director of the Springfield Vet Center. Jeff's friends Nick, Pablo, and Nathan helped carry his casket.

Debbie brought people to tears as she spoke. "On June 22, 2004, my brother, who's also my best friend, left the world that we all live in. My brother did not take his own life. It was taken from him when at twenty-one years old he left for Iraq and saw things that I cannot even imagine. He would come over to my place and tell me his thoughts and feelings in great detail and he always ended with 'You'll never understand.'"

Family members related to this sentiment, but the Marines present became confused. They had seen Jeff as a functional guy in Iraq whose problems arose back home. Was Debbie blaming *them,* or the Corps, for their comrade's death? At that time, early in the wars, people were not quick to make a connection between war experiences, PTSD, and later psychological problems. The Marines discreetly asked the funeral home director afterward if they would be welcome at the funeral the next day and were assured they would.

The funeral included a Catholic mass at the church where Jeff had been baptized, gone to his first confession, his first communion, religion classes, confirmation, and his sister's wedding. And now this. His flag-draped coffin was carried by Marines. Even more Marines from Jeff's Reserve unit showed up, in formal uniform.

As he watched the casket slide into the hearse, Kevin glanced at the full parking lot across the street near the town common. He recalled watching Jeff laughing and running from ride to ride at the Belchertown Fair, which took place each year on the common. The day's drizzly rain stopped, as did Kevin's tears, and their car pulled out into the procession. Kevin could no longer feel anything. The sounds of the other cars seemed so far away. A lump in his throat felt as if it would choke him. A police officer snapped to attention and saluted the hearse, starting Kevin's tears flowing again.

Jeff's "last convoy" picked up speed, heading to the cemetery. When it arrived, the grave plot seemed so small to Kevin. How could it contain him? Jeff was so energetic. His parents couldn't help but think about who he could have become and the wonderful family that he and Julie might have had.

People spoke. People cried. People went up to touch the casket one last time or to place flowers on it. The Marines performed the flag ceremony and presented the flag that had been on his casket to the Lucey family. The bugle blew "taps," the shots were fired, and the melodies of Peter, Paul and Mary singing "Where Have All the Flowers Gone" and "Day Is Done" floated on the day's breezes up to heaven.

PICKING UP THE PIECES

After the funeral, the family pulled together to face the facts that life would go on, but it would never be the same. The crazy, frantic efforts to deal with Jeff's behavior gave way to a quiet, sad, reflective period. Julie hung out on the back porch a lot in the months after Jeff died, talking with Joyce.

In an unnerving twist, suicide notes from Jeff kept turning up. They revealed the secrets of Jeff's ongoing inner battles. Joyce recalled times when she had found him writing letters or locked in his room, which was unusual. One letter had fallen behind the TV and was discovered during house cleaning. Another was in his room. Another under a cushion. The final note was written to his father warning him "don't go downstairs. Call the police," but Kevin had never seen it that night, and the state police took it without telling Kevin, as part of their investigation. The Luceys only learned of this piece of the puzzle months later.

The notes revealed Jeff's changing feelings and overall confusion. In one, he praised Julie as "a wonderful person" and said he wasn't worthy of her. Now she could have "a great life to look forward to." In several notes, he thanked his parents for their love and for giving him a happy childhood. He wrote in one that "no one could ask for a better more loving or supportive family but I continuously hurt them." Yet, he was about to do the thing he had promised never to do because it would hurt them so much. And he knew it. "I've done a great deal of thinking about how much this is going to hurt the family in general and for that I am truly sorry. I also consider the fact that I have continuously hurt the family and let everybody down, especially myself. I figure this will be one last hard blow instead of a continuing or continuous array of painful moments."

He apologized in one note for not making sense "but these pills can make my thoughts and beliefs come out wrong. I thought that maybe it was the alcohol for a while since I drowned my sorrows in a bottle for months on a daily basis, but I have been sober for almost a whole week, which truly is a lot more than it sounds, and yet I am still being swallowed by pain." These letters allowed a brief glimpse into the troubled inner-workings of a suicidal mind.

Sometimes I wonder if a veteran with PTSD, like Jeff, who has become dysfunctional, may see suicide as a form of "taking out" an enemy. Jeff's enemy was his weakened self. It seemed beyond repair, wounded on the battlefield of civilian life, holding back his own unit by being the weak link in the chain, holding back his girlfriend from moving ahead with her life because he wasn't worthy, and holding back his family because they were pulling their hair out over him. He was the guy who liked to help other people or drive around and enjoy himself and not need anything. But all of a sudden he was a bundle of needs. And I think he hated that about himself. Though part of him was consumed with these needs, another part of him had no tolerance for them.

FINDING THEIR VOICE

Kevin wrote a statement that was printed in the local newspapers: "On behalf of my family, we are grateful for the outpouring of support after the death of our son. . . . [We] hope that his legacy can be lessons learned for others. First we hope to all others in the depths of despair, there can be a way out. Beyond that we can only tell Jeff's story." He told of Jeff's enlistment, of not being "prepared for the ravages of war," of coming back a different person and ending long talks saying "You'll never understand." Kevin wrote, "I am not a Republican or Democrat, a liberal or conservative. I speak as a father who has lost a son. . . . There are huge costs to war. . . . My son was one of the walking wounded, those whose souls had been devastated. When the dead are honored for their service in the war, I wonder if my son will be among them. I know he gave his life, and he lost it in Iraq. I respect war veterans. I honor their sacrifice. My brother was a Vietnam Vet."

And thus began the Luceys' mission to tell Jeff's story in the hopes that others might reach a different outcome. But it didn't come easy. The family members were traumatized themselves. Joyce realized that Jeff used to tell them that "no one can understand," and that now she felt the same way. As she noted, "A simple task, such as going into a grocery store, seeing items that you would have bought, seeing the favorite foods that he loved, all of a sudden the tsunami of overwhelming sense of loss, grief, and sometimes even panic takes place and you look around and you just have to escape. You just have to leave."

But taking their grief public also promoted the healing process, Joyce would come to realize. "It's not something that we hide. I think the more you talk about it, the more you adjust to it. Even when we come home at night and have done a talk, we're kind of wiped. You have your tears. I think its cathartic, it does something to you. It really makes you realize that this happened.... At the beginning, it was easier; I was numb. Now, it can be harder because I'm not numb anymore." In the end, it gave some meaning to Jeff's death—their determined, hard work to destigmatize PTSD and recognize suicide victims as war casualties.

VETERANS EDUCATION PROJECT

Over the next couple of weeks, I talked with the Luceys off and on. In one of those conversations, I told them about a local organization called the Veterans Education Project (VEP). I told them that Gordon, the Marine Vietnam veteran with whom Jeff made a brief positive connection, was a speaker for the VEP and that the program was a forum for veterans and their families to publicly share their personal stories of war and homecoming. I said that the program had been founded several years after the Vietnam War and that it created forums for people to speak frankly about war realities.

Later, they learned that the VEP trains and supports volunteer speakers from different military eras, from World War II through Afghanistan, who speak in western New England schools and a wide range of public venues. The VEP has no political allegiance or position on any war. Its premise is that simply by hearing real stories from reflective individuals who have been in war, people will come to understand the truth of the battle experience. Speakers often point out ways that war is typically glorified or sanitized in movies or glossed over in the attempts by recruiters to persuade high school students to enlist. The VEP believes that the deepest memories and reflections of war often lie buried and unspoken. Its educational programs are designed to expose these truths. Questions and comments from the audience probe deeper and make every presentation a unique dialogue. (I portray the VEP's work in more detail in chapter 10.)

I was not sure what interest the Luceys might have in the VEP but thought it might provide some comfort to hear others speaking out. Soon after, Kevin called the program and arranged to meet with its directors, Rob Wilson and Susan Leary. Rob and Susan had listened to the stories of many veterans but never a story so fresh from a family in acute grief. They were moved but wondered what they could offer of value to the Luceys. For starters, they invited them to attend an event in nearby Northampton, sponsored by the American Friends Service Committee (AFSC), which featured a panel discussion about the impact of the Iraq War.

Kevin, Joyce, and Debbie went to the event, as did Jeff's friend Pablo, who was anticipating redeployment to Iraq. It was the first time I had met Pablo. The program's main speaker was Marine veteran Jimmy Massey, who served in Iraq and came to feel betrayed by the U.S. government's decision to invade that country. Accusing the U.S. military of war crimes in Iraq, Massey had been traveling around the country telling his story. The youngest in a long and proud line of military family members from Waynesville, North Carolina, he had been a gung-ho Marine for nearly twelve years before the Iraq War and had voted for George W. Bush in 2000. But he said that he changed his views after being ordered to shoot civilian demonstrators in Iraq. As he spoke in Northampton, his voice was strong, his points clear. He had my full attention, and he roused the audience. Because of his accusations, he would become a flashpoint for controversy on his speaking tour. But his candor resonated with the hundred or more activists and veterans present that night.

Shortly after, Kevin, Joyce, and Debbie showed up at the next VEP event, also featuring Jimmy Massey, at the public library in Amherst, my home town. I sat apart from them but wondered what they were feeling as the speakers talked about the hidden costs of war. The Luceys came just to listen—they were still in shock. But before it was over, Debbie found her voice, and during the question and comments period she stood up and described what she had been through. Her story gripped the audience and the panel. It was raw and highly emotional. She had a question for the panelists, but suddenly all the attention in the room was on her story, not theirs. It was clear that more would be heard from Debbie. After the event, the family talked with Massey, describing Jeff's thousand-yard stare, telling them "you'll never understand." Massey nodded.

Soon after, Rob Wilson reached out to the Luceys with a letter. "I hope that you met some individuals last night who share your concerns (as we at VEP do)," he wrote, "and who ultimately can support you and even work with you to give Jeff's story voice, so that his story becomes an agent of change that ultimately helps and supports both those returning from Iraq and their parents." The Luceys were a bit overwhelmed by the emotion of the events, but this invitation led to their becoming the program's first speakers portraying the experience of veteran families and loved ones. Further still, several years later they founded and co-led the VEP-sponsored Military Families Connect program, which offers ongoing support group meetings for military families.

As the Luceys allowed their story to be known, people reached back to them, for the most part, in very touching ways. Their policy became, "We will speak anywhere to anybody," and their ability to be candid was compelling. They told audiences, "Don't treat us as porcelain dolls. If you don't ask us the hard questions, you're insulting us." Jeff's story resonated with many people outraged at the impact of the war on our nation's young men and women. It gave a real face to a problem, PTSD among recent war veterans, that few Americans had thought about at that time.

Being public also took its toll, though. After Jeff died, his older sister Kelly said, "Don't be ashamed; let's put it out there." But after she read an online blog post stating that Jeff's parents had killed him by putting him in the VA against his will, and thus humiliating him, Kelly pulled away from the public dimension. She felt that comments by people who didn't know the facts just added insult to injury.

BOSTON AND DEMOCRACY NOW

In July 2004, just a few weeks after Jeff's death, a Veterans for Peace (VFP) convention was held at a university in Boston. The convention was held at the same time as the Democratic National Convention, where a famous Vietnam veteran who had become an antiwar activist, John Kerry, was being nominated for president. The Luceys were invited by VFP co-directors Charlie and Nancy Lessin. They met a psychiatrist there named Robert Jay Lifton, who is one of the people credited with lobbying for the inclusion of PTSD in the 1980 edition of the widely used *Diagnostic and Statistical Manual of Mental Disorders* (DSM). Lifton is also a well-known author and antiwar activist, who had played a role in the movement against nuclear weapons.

After the presentation, the group gathered in a large room where they sat in a circle. Everyone had the opportunity to introduce themselves and say why they were there. One by one, people mentioned that their loved ones were "over there" or had just returned. Then it came to the Luceys, the first to report that their loved one was gone. Joyce said Jeff's name and started sobbing. Kevin tried to say something. Haltingly, he said, "My son committed suicide a few weeks ago." It became real. A man named Fernando, who would become an ongoing friend and ally, approached the Luceys afterwards. He had lost his son in March 2003, at the very beginning of the war. His son was wounded and lay dying in a street for two hours during a firefight. Nobody could get to him, and he bled out.

The Luceys were asked to return to Boston the next day for a radio interview with Amy Goodman, the host of *Democracy Now*, a well-known national radio show. Goodman was in Boston to cover the Democratic convention.

During the interview, Kevin and Joyce depicted Jeff's time in Iraq, his downward spiral, their unsuccessful attempts to get help from the VA, and his suicide. Kevin described that "as time went on, he started watching various news programs and he started speaking up against the war and why it was being fought, why innocents were being killed. He couldn't merge his life with what he had seen and what he had gone through. And he started telling us, as time went on, a lot more of what he saw, what he saw Americans do."

Kevin mentioned finding the two dog tags that Jeff left on his bed on the day of the suicide and that Jeff associated them with killing two unarmed Iraqis. Goodman keyed in on this revelation. "What do you mean he was ordered to shoot them and they were unarmed? . . . Where did he kill them? In Nasiriyah?"

Kevin replied, "We don't know."

Joyce continued, "We don't have the whole story. He would just give bits and pieces. You would never get the full [story]. But he told his sister that he was just like five feet away from one of them that he had to kill. And he watched him die. . . . He never wanted to shoot."

Kevin added, "He had never shot a squirrel before."

Immediately after the radio show, the Luceys were directed into a TV studio and were interviewed on camera for Patricia Foulkrod's documentary *The Ground Truth* about the struggles of returning vets. As that interview ended, and they were about to leave, suddenly Amy Goodman came rushing in. She pointed out that what they had said about Jeff shooting an unarmed soldier was a war crime. She wanted to ask them more questions.

It was quiet for a couple days after the interview, but then suddenly the phone started ringing. The first few calls were from sympathetic listeners, including a woman who had heard the radio broadcast as she was holding her infant son. She said she couldn't imagine their grief. Other calls were sparked by the sudden concern about a possible war crime. Suddenly, antiwar activists, watchdog groups, and journalists had something to work with, and the military was on the defensive. The Luceys had not anticipated this development, as their focus was simply on telling Jeff's story as accurately as possible. Though the Luceys never requested an investigation, inquiries into Jeff's war experience were subsequently conducted both by the U.S. Marine Corps and by investigative reporter Christopher Buchanan with the PBS show *Frontline*.

Both concluded that some of Jeff's reports, in particular the shooting of the unarmed Iraqi men, could not be officially substantiated, although they conceded that they could not be absolutely refuted either. However, the Luceys found significant flaws in the investigation process. Remarkably, the Luceys were not consulted as part of these inquiries, which missed key details as a result. Thus, conclusions were reached based on limited and inaccurate information. For instance, Buchanan operated on the false assumption that these were prisoners being transported, when actually Jeff had said they were Iraqis on a roadside who were considered suspicious. The Luceys were also skeptical of the bias of the Marine investigation when the first statement they got back from it was that Jeff had never transported POWs. When the parents produced photos proving otherwise, they received a terse response acknowledging the inaccuracy.

According to the Marine Corps investigation, Jeff never went into Nasiriyah during the heavy fighting:

> *Some members of 1st Transportation Support Group were assigned to support 24th Marine Expeditionary Unit (Special Operations Capable) for the duration of offensive operations in Iraq. . . . Lance Corporal Lucey remained attached to 1st Transportation Support Group running general support missions for I MEF and was not part of the unit assigned to support the 24th Marine Expeditionary Unit (Special Operations Capable). . . . Lance Corporal Lucey did participate in a resupply mission in support of 2nd Battalion 2nd Marines (Ground Combat Element for 24th Marine Expeditionary Unit). While at their location he and other members of the convoy did assist in some troop moves for the infantry battalion. . . . At no time while with 2nd Battalion, 2nd Marines was Lance Corporal Lucey separated from other drivers nor was he observed or reported firing his weapon.* [24]

Sergeant Jonathan Braca, who had been part of the MEU mission, told the *Frontline* investigator that he remembered all eighteen drivers who participated, and who formed close bonds as a result. "Lance Cpl. Lucey was *not* a part of the MEU mission," he said.[25]

The Marines' investigation noted that "Lance Corporal Lucey was considered to be quiet and hardworking, overall a good Marine that made friends easily." A charismatic leader in Jeff's unit, Gunnery Sergeant Brian Fitzsimmons (known as Gunny Fitz), reported:

> *During my personal observation of L. Cpl. Lucey, he performed admirably. Any missions he went on that were inherently*

dangerous, he volunteered for. I trusted him. He made good, timely decisions for a Marine of his rank and training. I have no knowledge of him ever discharging his weapon, in any type of scenario. . . . I also know L. Cpl. Lucey did not go on any missions with me that imminent danger was briefed. L. Cpl. Lucey was with me during most of the actual conflict running general support missions for I MEF. Lance Corporal Lucey did participate in a resupply mission supporting 2nd Battalion 2nd Marines with me.

Light Truck Company operated throughout the entirety of I MEF's zone of operations, from as far south as the Iraqi-Kuwaiti border to as far north as Tikrit. During this time, there were numerous instances when elements of the Company would be gone for days at a time, comprising parts of countless spontaneously-created convoys. . . . As for Lance Corporal Lucey specifically, he was part of many of these convoys . . . The makeshift nature of many of the convoys prevents me from knowing exactly which convoys he was on, but to my knowledge at no time was L. Cpl. Lucey ever attached to a unit for any length of time without being in the immediate company of other Marines from Light Truck Company.

Frontline's Christopher Buchanan talked to members of Jeff's unit and looked at all available records. He concluded of Jeff's stories, "We don't think the stories are true and we can't say that they are absolutely not true, but our conclusion was that basically we don't think they happened."[26] Jeff's fellow Marines did not find the story of killing two Iraqis credible, and the dog tags probably did not come from those men in any case (most Iraqi soldiers, and all civilians, did not wear dog tags). Perhaps Jeff got the dog tags elsewhere but repurposed them in his mind to represent the two Iraqis he had killed, be it in reality or delusion.

The Luceys never pinned their broader concerns on the unknowable details of what exactly happened. They continued to believe that Jeff had no reason to make up the shooting stories. Who benefited from that story? Certainly it was not a war story to brag about but rather a source of shame for Jeff. Nor did Jeff appear to need a ploy to get people's attention or concern. An investigation revealing that Jeff was involved in a war crime would have just added pain to the Luceys' remorse.

Personally, I was in no position to make any decisions about the truth. Although I found some of what Jeff revealed as shocking, I believed him. Despite his drinking problem, he was always coherent when we spoke. There was nothing to be gained from his story of shooting two unarmed Iraqis under orders. This was not a tale of heroism; it was a painful confession from a tormented man. The story also matched and helped explain his extreme state of emotional distress. At the same time, the incident that ended "very badly" for the POW with the razor blade may have been traumatic enough in itself to account for his severe PTSD. Jeff's sporadic and sketchy references to his experiences illustrate his profound ambivalence about revealing his secrets. What few details he did offer were like leaks that he couldn't hold back. He alluded to there being much more that he couldn't tell. No doubt, guilt and shame held him back. No one who knew him got the impression that he was telling fabricated, exaggerated, or glorifying stories.

I find Jeff's story of shooting the two Iraqis believable. There are enough cracks in the investigation reports to allow that at one point he could have been out on a mission assigned to drive some sergeant he did not know. And they could have stopped, and in the heat of the war, this sergeant could have ordered that action. "All rules of engagement are off; shoot anything that moves," Jeff had said. What evidence would exist that it had ever happened? I asked Pablo, who was there driving trucks in the Nasiriyah campaign, whether he thought someone might have ordered Jeff to do that. "It's possible," Pablo answered. "It's very, very, very possible. A lot of times we are on our own on the road and stuff. . . . It definitely could have happened." I have worked with other veterans who have revealed, in confidence, that they killed in combat unnecessarily. One told me of a commander who directed him to "take care of" a wounded enemy in Afghanistan after they had captured and interrogated him. They had determined that he had detonated a bomb resulting in U.S. deaths. Emotions ran high in the wake of the incident. They found him hiding in a remote area, and after the questioning, the commander left the area so that there would be no witnesses. To say that a war crime can occur at the hands of U.S. Marines is not to impugn the whole Corps or the entire U.S. military. It is to acknowledge a reality. War is not "clean." We are outraged at atrocities committed by the enemy, but they happen on both sides.

Above and beyond PTSD (though often overlaid on it), such incidents create what Vietnam-era writer Jonathan Shay calls "moral injury" to the perpetrators, an assault on their very characters and belief systems.[27]

I accept that exactly what happened to Jeff is impossible to say. But I hold to the understanding that war is traumatic to combat troops, to support troops, and to civilians, and few of them come out the other end with clean, concise stories about their experiences. I'm a therapist, not a journalist, politician, or officer, and it is not my job to prove or disprove. The one person who knows for sure is gone.

In a sense, the controversy surrounding what Jeff experienced was another distraction for the Luceys to overcome as they sought to convey their core message. The Luceys never believed that PTSD is determined by how much you do or witness, nor did they believe that the traumatized person needs to justify his or her condition, but rather that different people are affected in different ways, and each story can best be understood by uncovering the unique meaning within that person. The bigger issue is the inevitable cost of sending young people off to war and how to care for them when they return. The military had focused on gearing up troops for battle but had not taken full responsibility for deconditioning them for civilian life.

At that time, in 2004, the people most sympathetic to the underside of war and the hidden consequences of combat were primarily Americans opposed to the Iraq War, especially veterans and military families against the war. These activists were not just "peaceniks." They had strong reasons to object to this war based on fabricated rationales and ill-considered consequences. Their opposition to the war would later gain wider national acceptance, but for now their voices were in the minority. In these communities, the Luceys found compassionate listeners and comforting friendships. There they found understanding and connection with others who could appreciate their pain and their outrage.

After speaking at events, the Luceys received many letters such as this:

> *We are very glad that we got to meet you yesterday and want very much to stay in touch. There are no words that can properly convey our sorrow at your loss. But please know that you are not alone. We are working to stop this war based on lies and to end the occupation so no more families have to go through the pain that you have experienced. Now more than ever, our voices must be heard. We have to speak out and say Bring Them Home Now!*

EYES WIDE OPEN

Among these antiwar groups was the American Friends Service Committee (AFSC), a Quaker peace group. On the first anniversary of the war, the AFSC's Chicago chapter created an exhibit called "Eyes Wide Open," which included about 500 pairs of combat boots, each with the name of a U.S. service member killed in Iraq. The exhibit was then sent out on tour, and with each new exhibit, the number of boots grew. In Philadelphia, shoes representing the number of Iraqi civilians killed were also included. The exhibit explained, "Families and friends gather around boots bearing names of their loved ones to mourn, to find solace in being with others in their grief. They attach photos, poems and other mementos to the boots bearing the names of their sons, daughters, fathers, and husbands." The project highlighted the costs of the war at a time when the U.S. government was not allowing media coverage of returning flag-draped coffins, was not providing any data on Iraqi civilian casualties, and was obscuring the war's financial costs.

The exhibit arrived in Amherst, Massachusetts, six weeks after Jeff's death. The Luceys were invited to participate, and they loaned Jeff's boots for the display. These were the first boots belonging to an actual service member, as opposed to the others, which were just symbolic. They were also the first belonging to a victim of the psychological wounds of war and the first suicide. The boots were laid out in a grid of rows and columns spaced about a yard apart. Jeff's brown boots were well-worn with no sign of shine. The laces were loose as if he could slip right into them again easily. Dangling from one boot was a laminated formal Marine photo of Jeff. From the other hung a photo from his high school yearbook. The boots sat next to flowers and an American flag.

At a boots exhibit fifteen months later, Kevin Lucey said:

Today we gather to remember each and every man and woman whom these boots commemorate as well as those who have died unknown and uncounted because of wounds—both physical and unseen—which ultimately claimed their lives be it in the hospitals of Germany or in the safe havens of their hometowns. These are solemn, somber, and reflective moments for the families and loved ones of those which these boots represent. They evoke cherished memories of their lives as well as serving as tragic reminders of their loss and the unrealized potential of what could have been . . . regardless of what set of political beliefs in which you may believe. We do not want the number of these boots to increase or the number of families to be traumatized by the true real horrors of war. . . . There have been over 2000 military deaths as of this date, six more yesterday alone—six more families that will feel stabbing pain and inconsolable grief—an untold number of emotional deaths and for some emotional scarring that will last a lifetime and ripple down through their families, friends and community.[28]

After Amherst, Jeff's boots became part of the traveling exhibit. The Luceys were invited to go to New York for the next installation in Central Park. The Luceys were moved by the power of seeing Jeff's boots in the big city. Another parent, Liz Sweet, from Washington, DC, learned of Jeff's story and contacted the Luceys. Her son had committed suicide in Iraq, and she wanted her son's boots right next to Jeff's. She brought her son's real boots and put them next to Jeff's, and then suddenly other veterans' parents brought their actual boots.

Joyce at "boots" exhibit with civilian shoes, 2005.

Without trying to, the Luceys were changing the feel of the exhibit and making it more real.

The Luceys hadn't even realized that the Republican National Convention was taking place in New York right then. Ironically, the Luceys had been in Boston during the Democratic convention and now were in New York at the Republican convention. There was a huge antiwar counter-rally, with celebrity speakers such as Danny Glover. One of the protestors, the mother of a veteran who had died in combat, told the Luceys forcefully, "You have to march. You've lost your son, you have to march." So they did. Debbie carried a little card of Jeff's face. She was approached by reporters to answer questions. Those interviews ultimately led to the PBS *Frontline* documentary, "The Soldier's Heart," which featured Jeff's story.

After the event, Debbie and another marcher named Jess went back to the hotel. Debbie was wearing buttons that said, "He's not my president" and the word "War" with a line through it. They got into the elevator with two well-dressed women. One looked at Debbie's buttons and said, "Oh, honey, you don't mean that." Debbie said, "Yes, I do. My brother is dead because of the president." Then the woman said, "Oh, I'm so sorry" in a sympathetic tone.

When they got off the elevator, Jess said, "Do you know who that was?" Debbie looked puzzled. "No, but I know she has a lot more money than I do."

"That was Dick Cheney's wife."

NEAR THE END of August, two months since Jeff's death, Kevin still hadn't returned to work. He had tried to go back a couple of times, but it was overwhelming. He dissociated frequently, feeling outside his own body looking in. He'd space out while driving and forget where he was. One day, he drove off with no direction and no intention of coming back, until a feeling turned the car around and guided him back home. He began to have anxiety attacks. On the first day he finally returned to work, he called Joyce to help calm his trembling hands. Kevin's own drinking increased, and he gained a lot of weight. Ativan, an anti-anxiety medication, made its way into the family medicine cabinet.

For Joyce, it was beginning to sink in that Jeff was really gone. She broke down in a TV interview and then said, "Please don't put this on TV. I don't want my daughters to see this." They didn't. Kevin had been writing a letter to George Bush when Jeff was alive. After Jeff died, he continued it. Joyce kept writing letters to Jeff. She wrote them on one pad of paper, one after another. She recalls how the buffer of shock began to melt as she realized that Jeff was not in Iraq. He wasn't sleeping somewhere else. His car would never come into the driveway again.

Debbie's journals from the time read, "Jeff is gone and I can't see him anymore. I can't even say the d-word." She would find herself telling people that Jeff was gone, and they would say, "Where is he, in Iraq?" People caught on when she couldn't answer.

Debbie kept thinking she could still call her brother. She imagined seeing Jeff everywhere. One night, a guy walked into a local pub, and she thought it was Jeff. She'd see a car that looked like Jeff's and raise her hand to wave only to feel the sharp pain of loss again. A memorial service was held at Holyoke Community College in the fall. A picture of Jeff was mounted in the hall. Again, Debbie saw someone at the service she at first thought was Jeff.

Nevertheless, the Luceys continued to have the courage to talk and answer any questions on the public stage, with reporters and, frankly, anyone who cared enough to ask. They were forthcoming, honest, and emotionally genuine. As they were invited onto panels, they were often paired with others who shared concerns about the impact of the war on our military personnel. They could see that they were not alone. They also learned about organizations like Iraq Veterans against the War, Veterans for Peace, and through Nancy Lessin and Charley Richardson formed a relationship with Military Families Speak Out. The Luceys were forced to develop a thick skin as they told their story. Debbie notes that "we began to realize that some people aren't going to say nice things once we put this out into the media." This realization fortified them for action.

THE MEDIA WAVE

The Luceys' story touched a nerve with the media. Television coverage included ABC, CBS, NBC, CNN, MSNBC, HDTV, NECN, and Channel 5 Boston. NPR interviewed the Lucey family. Newspaper coverage included the *Boston Globe*, *Boston Herald*, *New York Times*, *Los Angeles Times*, *Providence Journal*, *Newsday*, *Boston Phoenix*, *Chicago Tribune*, *New York Post*, *New York Daily News*, *New Republic*, *Daily Hampshire Gazette*, *Worcester Telegram and Gazette*, and *Springfield Republican*. Magazine accounts appeared in *Vanity Fair*, *Maxim*, *Rolling Stone*, *Newsweek*, *East Coast*, *Esquire*, and *Grazia*. International media coverage included Australia, Austria, Japan, Germany, Russia, Switzerland, Iran, England, Algiers, Italy, China, Canada, France, and Sweden.

Several documentaries covered aspects of the story, including *The Ground Truth: The Human Cost of War* by Focus Features, *The Soldier's Heart* by PBS *Frontline*, *Hidden Wounds* by NECN, *My War, My Story in Their Boots* by Wolfgang Pictures, *Over The Bridge* by Olivier Morel (French), and *When Jane and Johnny Came Marching Homeless* (being released in the United States in 2014). Two plays, several songs, and a number of poems were inspired by Jeff's story. More and more service members were returning from Iraq, and Americans were starting to learn about PTSD and suicide.

The Soldier's Heart aired on the second anniversary of the war. Despite the fact that *Frontline*'s assigned reporter called into question the specifics of some of Jeff's Iraq experiences, the documentary stood behind the Luceys' core belief that "something happened to Jeff" and wove his story into its exposé on the psychological impact of war.

The *Frontline* producer emphasized that the country was facing an enormous challenge. "In Jeff's case, he really didn't want to seek help," she said. "That is one of the major themes of our show. That it's great for the military to put all these programs and policies in place but if the soldiers aren't going to access them and seek help, there's a problem. It's the military culture."

Meanwhile, the more antiwar-oriented documentary, *The Ground Truth*, Patricia Foulkrod's film, was in production, and an early version aired in October 2004 just before the election. It focused on the costs of the war to those who had been sent to fight it. In a pre-release screening, two outspoken veterans led a discussion afterwards. One of them was First Lieutenant Paul Rieckhoff, an Army infantry platoon leader who had returned from Iraq in February and founded "Operation Truth." He would go on to lead Iraq and Afghanistan Veterans of America (IAVA) and advocate tirelessly for vets. Rieckhoff had graduated from Amherst College in 1998 and enlisted in the Army, transferred to the Army National Guard, and served a year in combat in Iraq.[29] In 2004, he served on veterans' advisory councils for New York City and New York State.

After the screening, Rieckhoff wrote the Luceys, explaining that Operation Truth was "a non-profit, non-partisan Iraq Vets group dedicated to telling the story about the war in Iraq from those who have served." He offered his organization's support to the Luceys, thus beginning an ongoing collaboration.

MILITARY FAMILIES SPEAK OUT AND GOLD STAR FAMILIES FOR PEACE

Kevin and Joyce went to Fayetteville, North Carolina, for the first national meeting of Military Families Speak Out (MFSO). It had about two thousand member families at that time and was growing. The blend of the organization's military connection, its opposition to the war, and its demand for better veteran care resonated with the Luceys.

At first, the Luceys felt awkward. "I remember sitting at a table and us not knowing anybody. I felt very uncomfortable," Joyce recalls. But then someone came over and said it was their honor to meet them, because she had just seen the *Frontline* documentary that had aired a few weeks earlier. She said she was so moved by the Luceys' story. "This is how we started mingling, beginning to feel like we were part of this whole thing together. I remember Charlie and Nancy . . . would tell us to go up and write on the board—one word that this organization means to you. People would put down things like 'support.'" Kevin and Joyce began to notice other parents with whom they had met over the preceding months, and soon they felt like part of the group. Joyce and Kevin were impressed that busy people—college professors, writers, ministers—had traveled to be together and share their families' stories, and how the war had affected them.

Joyce recalls that Fayetteville was in the heart of "military country," making it all the more meaningful when it was her turn to speak. As she stood on a stage before more than a thousand people, she found the resolve to tell her story.

Later, as Kevin and Joyce listened to the speakers, "all of a sudden this little shy woman starts blasting out" to the audience of thousands. She was a mother named Cindy Sheehan who was very outspoken about her son, Casey, who had died in Iraq. Like Joyce, she was there with her husband, and they made a connection. She wrote to Joyce later, "Your son was a casualty of this stupid, damn war as much as Casey was . . . and you are a Gold Star mom as much as I am."

"Gold Star" families are those that have lost a family member in war. They receive a special pin from the government. The Luceys were not initially recognized as a Gold Star family. The Luceys never asked to have the same status for suicide victims but found themselves welcomed by other Gold Star families they met nonetheless, like the Sheehans. They eventually sought some sort of designation for those who died as a result of hidden wounds. They felt that their son was a victim similar to someone who had been shot and killed. Cindy Sheehan had co-founded Gold Star Families for Peace, which was "dedicated to bringing our troops home before any other families need to qualify for membership." She welcomed the Luceys into her events over the coming months and years. For instance, the Luceys would join a panel presentation in Cambridge, Massachusetts, a few months later where Sheehan spoke.

In April 2005, the Luceys testified at a hearing before the Joint Committee on Veterans and Federal Affairs at the Massachusetts Statehouse. The hearing examined the impact of President Bush's FY06 Budget and the effects it would have on the federal Department of Veterans Affairs (VA) and on Massachusetts veterans.

The Luceys were heartened by the responses of some politicians. Senator Edward Kennedy acknowledged their pain in a letter, saying in part, "I believe our country should be providing clearer and more effective support for you. I've heard from many of you about the difficult practical issues you face, even though the prevailing view today is that support services and benefits are in place and accessible." Kevin also contacted an aide to his congressman, John Olver, to ask for help in moving forward an official investigation of Jeff's treatment by the VA. (I will describe this investigation and the reforms it sparked in chapter 7.)

MARCH ON WASHINGTON

In late August 2005, the Luceys heard about a "Bring Them Home Now" bus tour sponsored by MFSO, GSFP, Iraq Veterans against the War, Veterans for Peace, and Vietnam Veterans against the War, all grassroots efforts of military/veteran families. The tour headed out from Crawford, Texas, where Cindy Sheehan had camped out near the Bush compound, and was to arrive a few weeks later in Washington, DC, for a rally in late September sponsored by the large national umbrella group, United for Peace and Justice. Three buses took separate routes to DC with stops for speaking events along the way.

One bus came to Amherst. An interfaith religious service was followed by a brief ceremony and reading of the names of the Massachusetts service members who had died as a result of service in Iraq. Jeff's name was included. A portrait of Jeff was unveiled, the first in a "One Hundred Faces of War Experience" project by a local artist (I will describe this in more detail in chapter 10). The "Eyes Wide Open" exhibit of boots was set up again on the town common, and I attended the candlelight vigil service in the evening.

The Luceys went to DC for the big rally along with about three hundred other military families. As usual, Joyce and Kevin felt comfortable with the other families but a bit out of their element in the big political events. They participated in a candlelight vigil, during which families who had lost loved ones told their stories, and legendary folk singer Joan Baez sang "Amazing Grace." A candlelight procession to the Vietnam Memorial followed.

On another occasion that winter, Debbie joined a group of outspoken parents who had lost loved ones to the war. They tried to get to the Pentagon, which was open to the public. Debbie carried letters and pictures of Jeff, hoping to just drop them off and leave. Along the way, a group of counter-demonstrators jeered at the group. Debbie was spit at. A young woman said to Debbie, "My brother would hate me for wearing his picture." She called Debbie a disgrace. There was a life-size effigy of actress Jane Fonda hanging from a tree (apparently, she was still hated by some for her sympathy to North Vietnam during that war). Many police officers were present. At this time, about fifteen months after Jeff's death, the country's feelings about the war were changing, and strong feelings boiled on both sides. Less than a year earlier, President Bush had won reelection. A year into the future, the country would turn against him and the Democrats would sweep the 2006 elections. The period in between was an uncomfortable and unsettled time for those on both sides.

The military families marching for peace let the media know ahead of time, and reporters turned out. So did the police in riot gear. Debbie and the others were turned back from the Pentagon, and guards there refused to accept her pictures of Jeff. Debbie noted that one, however, took off his mask and looked sympathetic, and that meant a lot to her. Some of the parents were crying, hurt by those who jeered at them. One parent said, "Our kids died for you."

MITT ROMNEY

In October 2005, the Luceys joined MFSO members to speak with the Massachusetts governor, Mitt Romney, at the State House. The meeting was to focus on the National Guard, which the governor controls. They wanted Romney to call for National Guard members to return from Iraq and to take care of them when they returned. Romney supported a bill to increase death benefits for families of Guard members. With the war taking its toll, the Massachusetts National Guard was falling far short of its recruiting goals, and Romney had concluded that "we're going to have to improve our side of the bargain."

However, at the start of the meeting, Romney said to those who had lost children to war "I have five sons. I understand what you're going through." This attempt at empathy missed the mark. The Luceys felt envy, not comfort, since Romney's sons hadn't gone to war and were still alive.

Kevin and others suggested that the flag be flown at half-mast to honor those killed in the war and also proposed better screening for people who might be suffering with PTSD. But as the meeting went on and parents spoke, Romney became defensive. Debbie broke into tears and was ushered out despite wanting to stay. Shortly after that, the governor left the meeting.

SETTLING IN

The articles and documentaries about Jeff continued to draw interest. The Luceys began to hear from other families more often. Most of the calls were from loved ones of those who had committed suicide. No matter how drained they might be after the calls, the Luceys knew the importance of listening to people's stories. They wanted to help. The callers just needed someone to talk to.

In May 2007, the Luceys submitted written testimony for a hearing on PTSD, Traumatic Brain Injury (TBI), and other mental health concerns of veterans. The hearing examined emerging data and treatment trends to ascertain what initiatives were currently underway in Massachusetts to address long-term mental health consequences for veterans and returning service members and to determine what future steps Massachusetts could take to better serve its veterans. Among other points, the Luceys wrote, "What we have found is that the Federal Government, state governments and local governments were not and still are not in any way prepared for the returning veterans." They asked the committee to examine how the state's emergency services response system could better serve veterans, such as by not turning away vets using alcohol (as it had with Jeff). They asked for the use of veterans' agents, knowledgeable in the maze of federal and state resources, to advocate for veterans' needs. And they advocated for better service delivery and health care, for both veterans and their families.

In 2007, columnist Bob Herbert wrote about the Luceys in the *New York Times.* "The Luceys are more than just concerned and grief stricken. They're angry. . . . They want the war in Iraq brought to an end. 'That's the only way to prevent further Jeffreys from happening,' Ms. Lucey said."[30]

They also wanted better resources to care for those who returned from war. "We thought that if we told other people about Jeff they might see their loved ones mirrored in him, and maybe they would be more aggressive, or do something different than we did. We didn't feel we had the knowledge we needed, and we lost a child," Joyce said. She would later tell me, "We just don't want other parents to go through the hell that we've gone through. We went through it alone and it was horrible and it took its toll on all of us."

So on one level the Luceys were working to stop the war and oppose the president's policies, but on another level their work was far less political, more bipartisan. For example, after they spoke at Amherst College, a young Republican cosponsor of the event thanked them, saying, "It was very moving. I agree that the event transcended politics and partisanship, and I am proud to have added the College Republicans to the list of co-sponsors. I can say, without risk of hyperbole, that it was the most worthwhile event we've done in a long time."

As the months turned to years, and as the country became less divided by the war, and as the war wound down in Iraq—and, finally, Afghanistan—the Luceys' work gained traction. Their call to treat suicide victims as war casualties became more widely accepted. Their demand for better mental health resources for returning vets was widely echoed in many places high and low, from the U.S. military itself to local community organizations.

MY ACTIVITIES

At the same time the Luceys were speaking against the war and in favor of veterans' support, I had become active in my own way within the mental health community. I found opportunities to learn more about the needs of veterans and eventually partnered with the Luceys and trainers from the local VA and Vet Center to help educate mental health professionals about war trauma.

At the time, I had been trained recently in a powerful therapeutic treatment for PTSD called Eye Movement Desensitization and Reprocessing (EMDR), which I will describe in chapter 9. Sadly, Jeff was never stable enough to engage in EMDR though I had hoped we would get to that stage. I knew that EMDR had proven effective with war veterans and sought to improve my skills and experience working with veterans.

A year after Jeff's death, I joined with local mental health colleagues and sponsored the first of many trainings I would help produce for mental health professionals. About fifty EMDR therapists attended the training conducted by psychologist Susan Rogers. She and Steven Silver, her colleague from the inpatient PTSD Program at the VA Medical Center in Coatesville, Pennsylvania, had trained thousands of mental health professionals at VA, military, and civilian venues on issues of war trauma and had coauthored the book *Light in the Heart of Darkness*.[31]

Part of the training featured a panel that included myself, Kevin Lucey, and Jaime Perez, the clinical social worker from the Springfield Vet Center who had seen Jeff. Before the event, the three of us stood together for the first time. It was a solemn moment as we were aware of our common link. Yet we confirmed our common goal of raising therapists' awareness around veteran issues. Jamie was not asked to speak about Jeff but rather about his own experience as a therapist in Iraq. He had been back to Iraq since Jeff's death and served with troops in combat. His task was to try to "fix" the soldiers in three days and help them return to the field. He met with them individually and conducted many critical-incident debriefings. Jaime was stretched thin and described the strain on the limited mental-health resources in the war zone. During his last deployment in Iraq in 2009, Jaime was in one of ten mental health units. At that phase in the war, rather than traveling with military units, mental health workers were located in facilities away from combat. Some soldiers received three to seven days of hospital-based treatment before being sent back to their duties or back home. Jaime used EMDR and other strategies to help troops recover from traumatic exposure and to reduce the risk of compounding trauma in the war zone.

At this and a number of later trainings, the combination of the Luceys' story and my professional recommendations have motivated therapists to work harder and smarter at serving veterans. Joyce, Kevin, and I offered a presentation called *Return to Hell: Postwar Challenges for Veterans* to professionals in the medical, mental health, substance abuse, and criminal justice fields. Audience feedback was consistently positive and heartfelt, and demonstrated that community-based mental health professionals are hungry for information and strategies for helping veterans.

We offered suggestions for systemic changes in such areas as crisis intervention services, hospitalization, and public health policy. These included improved screenings for veterans at risk of PTSD, including risk assessment protocols; simultaneous treatment of PTSD and

substance abuse; better crisis intervention and access to hospitalization; and stronger family support services. We explained how to identify and understand PTSD symptoms in war veterans, internal barriers
to seeking help, secondary traumatization among family members, and
the limits of community response systems for traumatized veterans.
Many of the specific talking points of the trainings will be discussed
later in the book.

TAPS AND MORE

In recent years, the Luceys have formed a connection with one of the
largest and most successful groups helping families deal with military-
related losses, the Tragedy Assistance Program for Survivors (TAPS).
It was founded by Bonnie Carroll in 1994 after her husband died in an
Army plane crash. A service member herself, Carroll is a trained counselor and expert on grief and trauma. TAPS has now helped more than
40,000 family members and caregivers through free "peer based emotional support, case work assistance, connections to community-based
care, and grief and trauma resources." TAPS defines itself as "the 24/7
tragedy assistance resource for ANYONE who has suffered the loss
of a military loved one, regardless of the relationship to the deceased
or the circumstance of the death." The group has been a godsend for
families of military-related suicide victims, as it opens its arms to loved
ones of combat deaths, training deaths, suicides, and other military-
related tragedies equally.[32]

As Kevin Lucey said in 2013, "We went to a memorial service for
a person and one of the things that we shared with his family is that,
when you have a suicide that occurs, so many people run away from
you, because they don't feel comfortable, they don't know what to say.
Here with TAPS, . . . they run to you. They, among other organizations,
were our lifelines, and they saved our lives."[33]

The Luceys met Major General Mark Graham at an event for
military families in 2010 and later his wife, Carol Graham, at an event
focused on military suicide. The Grahams suffered the loss of one son,
an ROTC cadet, to suicide a year before Jeff's death. Their other son
was killed in action in Iraq eight months later. They are close allies

to the Luceys and have tirelessly dedicated themselves to suicide prevention.[34]

The fight against stigma and to treat psychological and physical wounds equally would be a long one, though. Presidential condolence letters to families of military fatalities became one flashpoint, as these letters were sent to service members killed on duty whether through combat, friendly fire, or accidents—but not if they committed suicide. As the TAPS director for suicide support put it in 2009, "These families already feel such shame and so alienated from the military and the country, a letter from the president might give them some comfort, some sense that people recognize their sacrifice. What better way to eliminate stigma?"[35] In 2011, President Obama reversed the policy for suicides that occur in combat zones, saying he was "committed to removing the stigma associated with the unseen wounds of war." However, the majority of military suicides, which occur after deployment (especially given the typical delay in the onset of PTSD symptoms), still produce no condolence letter.

The Massachusetts state government eventually responded to the Luceys' efforts. The Statewide Advocacy for Veterans Empowerment (SAVE) program was created and sponsored by the Massachusetts Department of Veterans Services in collaboration with the Department of Public Health. It included a mobile unit that would go anywhere any time to meet with a veteran in need to make services immediately accessible. After an assessment phase, they guided veterans toward other existing services. The Luceys' experience was the inspiration for this innovative program, and they were invited to the announcement of the program and continued to promote it publicly.

THE CEMETERY AND WAR MEMORIAL

Jeff is buried in Island Pond Cemetery in Ludlow, Massachusetts. It has been a very active shrine. Joyce visits the grave periodically and gathers what continues to be left there as reminders that Jeff's friends still think about him: Empty bottles of Jeff's favorite drinks. Handwritten notes. The lyrics from the Shinedown chorus.

At one point, the town asked the Lucey family to remove all these items. Joyce wrote back,

I'm writing this from the heart of a mom. . . . Grief is a difficult road to travel—we all handle it differently. For my family having memorabilia that remind us of Jeff . . . make it a little easier to cope with this unacceptable loss. . . . Having been able to express our profound loss in this way has helped us survive—for this I will always be grateful. My two-year-old granddaughter, a niece who was born after his death, enjoys playing with the Red Sox ball at his grave. She is too young to understand but she connects a young man in a picture to this cemetery. I would hope before policies are implemented, the emotional impact this has on those who make a daily visit would be taken into account. In this world of advanced technology and change in the name of progress, I believe we are losing touch with our humanity and our compassion towards one another. . . . We feel that you as a board are at a crossroads and can either make this cemetery sad, cold, and depressing or a treasure filled with memories and love.

In 2008, the town of Belchertown dedicated a new war memorial on the town common, joining memorials from the Civil War, World War II, and Vietnam. A simple sculpture of a pair of boots and rifle with a helmet on the stock, it lists the names of twenty-three Belchertown men who served in the Middle East since the 1991 Gulf War. The memorial reads "Belchertown Honors Our Veterans Who Served In The Middle East Wars." The name of one man, killed by an IED in Iraq, is followed by a star.

The Luceys learned about the effort to build this memorial and contacted the commander of the local Belchertown Veterans of Foreign Wars (VFW) to see if they could make a donation and if Jeff could be recognized as part of it. He responded, "Sure, he can be on it," but added crisply, "but he's not getting a gold star." The Luceys were startled by what seemed like a prepared answer to a question they had not asked. It got worse when the commander's stance was reported in the local newspaper. The Luceys were still in the early stages of grieving, and they had not asked for any special recognition, though later they felt that some recognition that Jeff had died with war-related wounds would be fitting. The Luceys were hurt by this response and felt offended. A standoff developed, and as a result Jeff's name is still not on the list of veterans on the memorial. To get on it, the Luceys would have to fill out paperwork, but first they wanted a more welcoming gesture of respect from the VFW.

So ten years later—in total contrast to organizations like TAPS that support the loved ones of *all* military-related fatalities—Jeff's hometown not only doesn't recognize him as a victim of war but has omitted the memory of his service altogether from the spot where the names of the other local war participants are chiseled in stone on the town common.

The memorial stands in front of the United Congregational Church (UCC) of Belchertown. Each year, at a Memorial Day service, the twenty-three names on the plaque are solemnly read aloud. One year, after the last name was spoken, the minister from the UCC church called out, "and Jeff Lucey!"

chapter 7

FORWARD MARCH—REFORMING THE VA AND PREVENTING SUICIDE

ALTHOUGH THE LUCEYS found community among military families against the war, their greatest influence was in pushing for reforms to the VA and military systems that take care of returning service members. They had little success in getting the government to "bring the troops home," but some success in getting the government to support vets when they did get home. After ten years, the reforms still don't go far enough, but they are extensive. They include better psychiatric evaluation and monitoring, creating a veterans' treatment culture that welcomes Iraq and Afghanistan veterans, increased engagement with family members and community care providers, improvements in treatment protocols, and the creation of suicide prevention coordinators at all VA hospitals. Quite possibly, if today's systems had been in place when Jeff returned from Iraq, he would still be alive.

THE VA INVESTIGATION

While the Luceys did not know at the time that suicides would be a signature mark of these wars, they knew something was wrong. They wanted to change the system. They saw that veterans were having to adapt to the existing and inadequate response system. Instead, they believed that the system should adapt to the needs of the veterans.

To start with, the Luceys requested the medical records from Jeff's treatment at the VA Medical Center (VAMC). They wanted a full psychological autopsy and an analysis of response system failure. They received no response initially, and when they pushed the matter, the VAMC claimed a Freedom of Information Act exemption. The Luceys began to feel that they were being "handled."

Around that time, after one of their speaking events, they met Chris Wyman, one of Senator John Kerry's staff members. At his suggestion, they wrote Kerry asking for assistance. They explained that their son had committed suicide after they twice attempted to get the VAMC to address his issues. They enclosed an article that had been sent to them suggesting the VAMC had been short-staffed. "We would request that someone examine the records for failures within the system—both the military and the Veterans Administration policies. . . . What happened to Jeffrey and our family should not happen to any other person and family."

Senator Kerry called for an investigation, which was carried out by the VA's Office of Inspector General (OIG) and Office of Healthcare Inspections.[36] The investigation was extensive and thorough, in my opinion. I was interviewed as part of the investigation and have read the transcripts from interviews with the primary professionals involved at the VAMC. The Luceys' concerns were heard, and difficult questions were asked. The investigators obtained and reviewed Jeff's medical records (electronic and paper) pertaining to his care at the medical center and reviewed quality-management and administrative records, including a "Root Cause Analysis and the psychological morbidity and mortality review that were performed after the medical center was informed of the patient's suicide."

Beyond the specifics of Jeff's case, the investigators reviewed the "medical center policies governing the evaluation and management of dangerous, violent, and suicidal behavior; psychiatric treatment plans; outpatient mental health discharges and failure to report to appointments; assessments specific to detoxification admissions; assessments specific to psychiatric admissions; and assessments of patients receiving outpatient mental health services."

The revelations about Jeff's treatment were disturbing, as they showed strong evidence he was in acute distress but a weak response to his needs. The discharge summary from the VA, after his stay over Memorial Day weekend, indicated a diagnosis of depression and substance abuse, with "severe" life stressors. Records from his initial assessment stated that he was at risk of self-harm or suicide and specifically mentioned that Jeff had indicated suicidal strategies including "to OD, hang himself or suffocate himself." His suicide risk at discharge was rated as "medium." Yet, neither the Luceys nor I were informed of Jeff's disclosures.

Jeff's records from the Vet Center on June 15 mentioned details including "drinking, nightmares, dressed in fatigues, suicidal, carrying knife, assaultive, threatening." They noted that he suffered from "disturbing and recurrent memories from traumatic experiences while in Iraq. Sleep problems, issues with alcoholism, anger problems, auditory and visual hallucinations, racing thoughts." Also, "recent suicidal thoughts though he denied current ideas/plans." When asked about traumatic events, Jeff had indicated "seeing children be killed and run over, a friend got attacked by POW." The records documented his abuse of alcohol since returning, along with a family/significant other relationship that "has been rocked," and difficulty in school. Clearly the VA was well aware of what shape Jeff was in. Records also noted that Jeff had, in fact, indicated that he was "willing to accept help."

Records documented the call from Kevin: "My son showed me where he was thinking of hanging himself." And the response: "I advised father to call the police for assistance." And Kevin's fear that Jeff would make good on threats of "trouble" if police arrived. When Jeff himself came on the phone, the VAMC recorded, he said that "his superiors in the Marines have told him his life will be ruined if he leaves reserves. Talked about vet feelings that there is no one who he believes can help him or cares enough to help him." Finally, "talked again with dad, who had listened to that side of the phone conversation, stressing that if he felt concern for his son's safety he should call police."

The investigation looked at the complicated issue of involuntary commitment. It reviewed Massachusetts law and explained that involuntary commitment for mental health reasons is a highly controversial and legally complex concept. On the one hand, the state has a responsibility to protect its people and society at large from dangerous and unstable people. The state also has a responsibility to care for those whose mental illness renders them unable to care for themselves. At the same time, the state must protect and respect individual civil liberties and provide care through the least restrictive treatment alternatives or environment. In Jeff's case, they believed that the VA medical center was within its rights to apply an involuntary admission for Jeff on his first visit to the hospital.

Regarding Jeff's four-day stay at the hospital and the care that he received, the investigators criticized the fact that Jeff did not have daily psychiatric attention. The fact that he was there over a holiday weekend did not lessen his need for daily attention and collaboration among psychiatric staff members. Had staff been available, Jeff's special observation status (because of suicidal ideation) could have been adjusted, such as to allow smoking breaks, and he would have felt less like a prisoner. The report determined that his discharge on the fourth day was appropriate, stating that the behavior he was exhibiting by then did not justify the hospital's applying for a court-ordered commitment.

The report commented on the impact of the "ward milieu." It cited the National Center for PTSD's Iraq War Clinician Guide, which indicates that "in the treatment of chronic PTSD, veterans often report that perhaps their most valued experience was the opportunity to connect in friendship and support with other vets. This is unlikely to be different for returning Iraq War veterans, who may benefit greatly from connection both with each other and with veterans of other conflicts." This certainly was not Jeff's experience. The report noted that there were no other Iraq-era veterans to whom he could relate. It speculated that this may well have influenced his request for discharge following his involuntary commitment and his reluctance to be read-mitted later.

The report criticized the after-care provided to Jeff and his family. While the investigators did not charge the hospital with professional negligence, they indicated that the hospital should have invited the family to a discharge planning meeting, which would have provided "an opportunity to further discuss treatment options, enhance communication, and to clarify patient and family concerns. In addition, this type of meeting might have provided an opportunity to facilitate greater patient receptivity and 'buy-in' for additional VAMC treatment options."

The report indicated that communication with me as Jeff's "outside therapist" as well as with his primary care physician would have been "preferable," but Jeff had not signed an authorization for release of information. In my view, he didn't sign because he wasn't asked to after he had calmed down from his initial intake. I could have communicated insights to staff, and would have benefited from their impressions of him. Crucially, I might have learned about the community-based Vet Center, which neither I nor the Luceys knew about until the VA thought to mention it weeks later. That said, today I would initiate a call to the VA without waiting to hear from them.

Regarding Jeff's trip to the VA a week after his weekend stay, the investigators found that "clinical staff appeared genuinely concerned" but did not take the extra step to call the Psychiatrist Officer of the Day (POD), who "was the best equipped to take ultimate responsibility for the final determination as to whether the patient could be admitted against his will" and should have been consulted. The report also criticized the lack of follow-up after that failed attempt to get help for Jeff, until Joyce called ten days later and first learned of the Vet Center as an alternative. Clearly, at that time the VA did not have in place the necessary procedures to effectively handle cases like Jeff's and the many that would follow.

With an eye toward reform, the OIG report recommended that the POD should be involved with all cases in which suicidal or homicidal ideation is an issue; that the VAMC clinical staff leadership re-evaluate admission criteria for newly diagnosed PTSD patients to the specialized inpatient PTSD program; and that newly admitted voluntary and involuntary patients be evaluated by a psychiatrist on a daily basis, including on weekends and holidays.

Coming early in the wave of returning veterans from Iraq, the OIG report played a crucial role in initiating reforms related to veterans' treatment. Beyond the VA, the report was distributed to the Senate and House Committees on Veterans' Affairs, the Senate and House Appropriations Subcommittees on Military Quality of Life and Veterans Affairs, and the Senate and House Committees on Government Reform, as well as the National Veterans Service Organizations and the Government Accountability Office.

All recommendations were accepted by the local VAMC along with the report's action plan deadlines for implementation. To their credit, the VAMC had already made voluntary changes to policies and procedures after Jeff's death. A new policy called for a social worker to be assigned to serve as the point of contact for the treatment of all Iraq veterans. The social worker was to be available to see veterans immediately in urgent situations and within one to two weeks of initial presentation in nonurgent situations. A patient representative was to be more clearly identified as the point of contact for administrative and other concerns for Iraq veterans. All staff who might have contact with an Iraq veteran were offered education regarding the different program options for veterans.

All on-call physicians were instructed to call the POD regarding potential admissions, emphasizing the need to make such a call when a decision not to admit a patient was under consideration. This practice was reinforced by a memorandum from the chief of staff. If any nonadmissions occurred during off-hours, the psychiatry day clinic was to be notified so that they could make a follow-up phone call to these patients the following day to inquire about their status and to offer further services. Also, a mental health clinician was designated as a liaison to the Vet Center to facilitate better communication between the two systems. Plans were underway to redesign the PTSD inpatient unit's treatment program to increase access for recently diagnosed PTSD patients and to concurrently treat substance abuse and PTSD.

These reforms would gradually work their way out across the sprawling VA system, which is one of the largest federal agencies in the country with more than 200,000 employees.

SUING FOR CHANGE

The Inspector General's report confirmed many of the Luceys' concerns about systemic problems in the VA response protocols. Dramatic as these reforms appeared, the Luceys did not rest. They filed a lawsuit against the VAMC. Their assumption was that the U.S. government could not be sued for a financial settlement. Instead, they sought an acknowledgment of responsibility and assurances of changes in policies and procedures in the treatment of veterans. They were never interested in targeting individual professionals.

They hired Cristobal Bonifaz, an intelligent and personable attorney with a passion for cases with a larger social value. He had worked on the Exxon Valdez lawsuit. Bonifaz had heard the Luceys' story when he attended a panel presentation, and Kevin had been the last person to speak. The crowd was silent after he finished but then erupted in applause. Kevin tried to leave immediately afterward, but a man came up to him with tears in his eyes expressing his sorrow for what they'd been through. It was Bonifaz. When they found out later that he was an attorney, they spoke with him about taking on the case.

Lucey v. United States charged the VAMC with three counts of wrongful death: 1) negligence in failing to have a Psychiatrist of the Day observe, evaluate and treat; 2) failure to provide proper training of psychiatrists, physicians, nurses, orderlies and employees; and 3) negligent supervision and monitoring of health care providers. Many of the issues in the OIG investigation came up again. I was deposed as part of the fact-finding process.

In the end, from a legal perspective, the weakest link in the VAMC defense was that when Jeff returned for his second visit to the VA, obviously still in distress and with a clear history of suicidality, no psychiatrist was called in to complete an assessment. An expert witness on the Lucey side testified that the standard of care dictated that Jeff should have been examined by a doctor before leaving the parking lot that day, as the OIG report had also recommended. An expert on the government side counter-testified that the VA had met the standard of care.

Midway through the depositions, the attorney for the government sent a letter to the Luceys including a settlement offer. The letter expressed "deep sorrow" for the Luceys' loss and "acknowledg[ed] that Jeffrey's suicide while under VA care was a tragedy for the VA and the individual care providers. But it also spawned a number of important changes in the hospital's procedures and outreach to Iraqi veterans." The letter pointed to the hiring of suicide prevention coordinators, new counselors for the Vet Centers, and advocates for the severely wounded. "As you know, Jeffrey was among the first Iraqi veterans to seek treatment at the Northampton VA. VA, both nationally and locally, has been challenged to appreciate and meet the health care needs of veterans returning from the conflicts in Iraq and Afghanistan. Jeffrey's case among others fostered awareness and led to improvements . . ."

The letter included a $350,000 settlement offer, which was accepted in January 2009. The Luceys felt their points with the local VAMC had been acknowledged. More importantly, they could see that reforms were spreading across the system.

In 2007, a memo from a top VA official instructed directors of the Veterans Integrated Service Network (VISN) to implement initiatives to upgrade services. They were to ensure that facilities make arrangements for twenty-four-hour crisis and mental health care availability and that an on-call mental health specialist should be available to crisis staff either in person or by phone. In addition, they were to ensure that all nonclinical staff who interact with veterans receive mandatory training about responding to crisis situations involving at-risk veterans, including suicide protocols for first-contact personnel. All health care providers were to receive mandatory education about suicide risks and ways to address them.

The memo emphasized that a requirement of sustained sobriety should *not* be a barrier to treatment in specialized mental health programs for returning war veterans. In addition, a bi-directional information exchange was to be set up between the VA and the military for patients with mental illness either entering the VA system or leaving it for redeployment to active-duty status. Finally, a centralized mechanism was established to review ongoing suicide prevention strategies; to select among emerging best practices for screening, assessment, and treatment; and to facilitate system-wide implementation to ensure a single VA standard of suicide prevention excellence.

A survey of VA facilities identified some innovative strategies, including the creation of a separate waiting room for women seeking treatment for sexual assault, an Iraq War "Combat Stress Group" that welcomes walk-ins, and the establishment of a "one-stop shopping" Mental Health Access and Referral Clinic to help place patients in appropriate programs on the day that they request service. About 85 percent of responding facilities reported implementing strategies to reduce the stigma associated with pursuing mental health or substance abuse treatment. New language was being developed to reduce resistance to seeking help. The concept of a "recovery model" was formulated to foster hope for the future and to counter growing expectations of chronic impairment and disability.

At the time, only 20 percent of facilities reported implementing community-based suicide prevention programs. Among those that did was the New Hampshire National Guard base, which had developed an aggressive outreach program. Immediately upon return, personnel there were contacted by other National Guard members to welcome them home and provide some literature. Two weeks later, they were contacted again by Vet Center personnel offering support. The program had already screened eight hundred Guardsmen, of whom 15 percent initially stated they wanted help. Creators of this program were well aware of Jeff's ordeal and solicited the Luceys' input as part of the program's creation. They learned that reaching out to family and community members was vitally important in reaching veterans who may themselves be reluctant to seek or accept help with mental health issues.

Within the VAMC, efforts were underway to implement a system-wide early intervention screening for depression, PTSD, and substance abuse, to be completed by primary care providers. Screening tools were improved with the qualifying statement that "despite some underlying commonalities, suicide and suicide attempts result from the complex interaction of a constellation of biological, psychological and social factors that manifest themselves within specific cultural and situational contexts." Ultimately, the VA validated that an in-depth, face-to-face clinical interview was the best way to screen and assess for suicide risk.

Strategies for tracking at-risk patients to ensure that they received timely and appropriate care were underway. Half the responding facilities reported having implemented strategies to target periods of increased risk for suicide. One facility reported ascertaining the anniversary of traumatic events in the initial psychosocial assessment and then incorporating this information into the individual treatment plan. Thirty percent of the facilities had begun electronically tracking veterans at risk for suicide, classifying patients into high, medium, and low suicide risk categories. This evidence-based risk assessment prompts the clinician regarding various known risk factors.

A SUICIDE PREVENTION COORDINATOR

One of the recommendations that came out of the investigation into Jeff Lucey's suicide was that a suicide prevention coordinator be appointed at each VAMC hospital nationwide. These coordinators oversee suicide prevention strategies, including the identification of veterans at high risk; coordination of enhanced care when needed; education of providers, veterans, families, and community members about risk factors and warning signs for suicide; and offering treatment options.

Ted Olejnik, a licensed clinical social worker, was appointed to that position at our local VAMC, where Jeff had sought treatment. Olejnik is a Vietnam veteran who served twenty-four years of active duty with the U.S. Air Force and began treating military combat stress in 1987. He treated troops from Iraq when stationed in Germany before transferring to Massachusetts to accept this position.

Ted and I have worked closely as colleagues since his arrival and jointly led trainings of mental health professionals on topics including military PTSD, suicidality, substance abuse, and EMDR therapy. I spoke one afternoon with Ted about military-related suicides and the changes in VA procedure since Jeff's death.

He noted that in Germany in 2007, "I first began to notice this tremendous increase in suicidal ideation and suicide attempts amongst the soldiers that I was working with who had been in the Iraq War. It was before I became a suicide prevention coordinator working for the social work and mental health services in Germany. I noticed how little emphasis was being placed on it. People were dismissing the severity."

Ted realized that he could identify the risk factors connected to how military personnel were managed post-deployment. "I learned that 90 percent of those who commit suicide have a dual diagnosis of PTSD with either substance abuse or some kind of mental health issue, most commonly, depression. That's a high risk factor that we have to key in on."

In his current position, Ted can highlight these risk factors in a veteran's medical record to help keep tabs on people who might be at risk for suicide, regardless of whether they are coming in demanding help. "If a veteran is assessed for suicidality by anyone in the VA medical system, there is a mandate that they be seen four times within the first month for a minimum of once-a-week help as a measure to keep them safe. An electronic flag is attached to the medical records so that each time he or she has contact with a health professional, that professional is aware that the veteran is deemed a suicide risk. We then follow the veteran closely." After three months, the health personnel review and assess risk, keeping the flag in place if warranted.

Veterans are aware of the flag and have to agree to have it in their file "because they may worry that there is a stigma attached to it. We don't want to keep the flag on unless it's necessary." Clinicians talk with the veteran and explain the rationale, and Ted meets directly with the flagged vets. If a patient opposes flagging because of fears of stigmatization, a staff committee meets to assess the case and make a recommendation on whether to keep the flag. "In practice, to this day,

I can think of only one person who refused the flag. Once they understood the concerns behind it and trusted that the staff was concerned with their well-being, they accepted it."

The clinicians try to reduce any stigma around mental health and especially suicidal thoughts, but "unfortunately," Ted says, "those with the greatest sense of stigma or shame are the people who won't even seek out mental health treatment. They think they should suck it up, just not be a baby anymore."

But, he continues,

> . . . the underlying issues that lead to suicide can never be addressed while a person is wrestling with the stigma. An example we had in Germany was one soldier who had already returned from Iraq and was ready to be redeployed. The soldier went onto the shooting range where he had to reach a qualification standard. While shooting he told someone that he was having flashbacks of combat experiences. He was distracted but was also very nervous about missing the target. He wasn't shooting very well. The squad leader started yelling at him. He said, 'Your shooting is making us all look bad!' The soldier asked for permission to go to the bathroom to relieve himself. In the military, you're taught to take the weapon with you wherever you go. He sat on the toilet, put the barrel under his chin, put it on full automatic and leaned on it. There was an investigation and the case was referred to me. It was clear to me that PTSD was affecting his shooting. The shooting itself literally triggered his memories of using a gun and all that had meant to him. Being screamed at by the squad leader must have induced old shame. On top of that, his coping skills were depleted.

Ted educates family members of veterans as well as professionals to be more aware of the underlying risks for suicide—conditions that statistically have been linked to suicide and thus, if identified, can alert others to the additional safety concerns for that veteran. These include depression; PTSD; bipolar disorder; substance abuse; medical illness; chronic pain; and a major loss such as a relationship breakup, a job loss, or financial setback. Other risk factors include a past suicide attempt, a family history of suicide, firearms in the home, local epidemics of suicide ("copycat" cases), and impulsive or aggressive tendencies. In Jeff's case, for example, PTSD, depression, alcohol, and relationship troubles were all indicators of a greater risk.

People who have previously tried to take their own lives are forty times more likely to commit suicide than those who have never tried before. A prior attempt may indicate the individual's acceptance of suicide as an alternative to life. When asking about prior suicidal behaviors, a clinician wants to ask what happened, how and when it happened, and why the person is still alive.

Risk factors increase or decrease depending upon personal resources, which include having a satisfactory job; adequate finances; a place to live; caring family or friends; access to psychological or medical help; and memberships in churches, clubs, or other social institutions. Strong values against suicide and skills in problem solving also reduce risk. Jeff had several of these elements in his favor.

Painfully, the aftermath of suicide often involves 20/20 hindsight. "I never saw it coming" is a genuine response of many. Below is a list of common warning signs of suicidal thoughts or plans. Some are obvious, although others may be surprising. With regret, I highlight Jeff's many warning signs in bold.

Warning signs of suicidal thoughts or plans:

- **Talking or writing about suicide, death, or self-harm directly or indirectly**
- **Expressing belief that life is meaningless/hopeless; no reason for living**
- **Sudden/unexplained improvement in mood after being depressed**
- **Increased agitation**
- **Neglecting appearance**
- If on medication, stopping medication and/or hoarding medication
- **Hoarding alcohol**
- Buying a gun; trying to get pills, guns, or other ways to harm self
- Cleaning a weapon that a person may have as a souvenir

- Giving away money/possessions
- **Change of interest in religion**
- **Isolating from friends/family; withdrawing from relationships**
- **Defensive speech; "you wouldn't understand," etc.**
- **Discontinuation of making eye contact or speaking with others**
- **Rage, uncontrolled anger, seeking revenge**
- **Acting in a reckless or risky way**
- **Feeling trapped, like there's no way out**
- Becoming overprotective of children
- Guarding the house; obsessively locking doors, windows
- Calling old friends, particularly military friends, to say goodbye
- Spending spree; buying gifts for family and friends "to remember me by"
- **Visits to graveyards**
- **Obsession with news coverage of the war, the military channel**
- **Wearing the uniform or part of it (e.g., boots)**
- Talking about how honorable it is to be a soldier
- Sleeping more (sometimes the decision brings peace of mind, sleep)

Risk factors and warning signs cannot provide definitive information about a person's inner experience, but they can cause someone to pay closer attention.[37] When trained professionals see warning signs, especially when combined with risk factors, there are important steps to follow. Ted teaches the QPR response protocol (Question, Persuade, and Refer) to all staff members who come into direct contact with VA patients. This and other information that follows is presented to provide the average reader with insight into professional procedures and is not a substitute for full training.

When risk factors are identified, *questions* can illuminate the veteran's condition. Some are indirect, such as, "Do you ever wish you could go to sleep and not wake up?" Others are quite direct, such as, "Are you thinking about hurting or killing yourself?", "Have you made a specific plan? What is it?", "Do you have access to . . . (a means of completing a suicide plan)?", and "What are the reasons you would not follow through on these thoughts?"

If these questions show reason for concern, the next step is to *persuade* the veteran to use support resources, with questions such as, "Will you go with me to see the counselor?", "Will you let me make an appointment with . . . ?", or "Will you promise me . . . ?"

If there is immediate risk, the protocol calls for staying with the veteran and making an immediate *referral* for services, including an escort to mental health care or the emergency room. The family is included in this process whenever possible.

Ultimately, a full assessment by a trained clinician covers different factors, such as present circumstances, recent changes for the worse, and physiological changes such as disturbed sleep or lack of interest and pleasure in daily things. Increases in crying, emotional outbursts, withdrawal, alcohol or drug misuse, and recklessness are reason for concern. Oddly, periods of sudden calm after a long period of struggle, especially combined with putting affairs in order, are also warning signs, as I now understand may have been true for Jeff.

Ted reviews three factors to estimate *acute* suicide risk—the person's current suicidal plan, prior suicidal behavior, and available support resources.

A client's suicide plan includes the choice of a method, preparation to carry out the plan, and a time frame for completing the act. The more detailed the plan, the greater the risk that the plan may be carried out. Perhaps surprisingly, Ted finds that most people who are thinking about suicide will openly and honestly share the details of their plans when asked directly. If someone will not tell the details of the plan, it is best to assume that he or she has planned it in detail.

Ted emphasizes the importance of developing an effective "safety plan" with a suicidal client, noting that it should go beyond a simple statement by the patient that he or she will not act on suicidal impulses. His plans build off a worksheet on which the patient checks off factors that may increase his risk, such as drinking problems, relationship issues, etc. Ted then helps veterans identify experiences that "trigger" suicidal thoughts. "We want to help them identify stressors, primary triggers and secondary triggers such as the anniversary of somebody's death, financial problems, or things of that sort. We want to make sure that the person has coping skills and, if not, begin to help them build skills. Then we guide them to come up with a safety plan that includes how they are going to manage risk factors including medications, and what they will do if they have any suicidal thoughts. We get their physical address and phone number." Ted provides the person with a copy of the written safety plan and keeps a copy in his or her medical record.

Ultimately, the clinician wants to *contract* with the person to reduce the immediate risk. This involves getting the person's agreement to a plan of action, which includes a commitment to participate in ongoing treatment. Developing a solid safety plan is a delicate process of building the person's trust in the value of staying alive, a realistic plan that covers as many challenges and contingencies as possible, and their commitment to stay safe by using the plan. To solidify the commitment, it is generally useful to have the person repeat the agreement to stay safe and avoid self-harm.

A clinician seeks to be a strong force in building the plan with the client but is careful to never assume responsibility for the person's life. Perhaps, at some point, a clinician's desire for the person to live on may be higher than the person's own, but ultimately professionals can only do their best to create conditions for this to happen.

A plan should identify resources to seek twenty-four-hour emergency support as a backup for when the steps of the plan for action do not ensure enough safety. Good plans also include suicide-proofing the person's environment. This may mean ensuring that firearms are locked up or surrendered, that drugs and medicines are safely out of reach, and that any preferred method of harm is not available.

"In the last four years, roughly six hundred people have been flagged," Ted notes. "Over the four years, we've had about five completed suicides." That's the kind of system now in place, not perfect but well ahead of what was available to Jeff Lucey at the VA in 2004.

Ted adds, "The bad news about suicide prevention is that those most at risk for suicide tend not to self-refer for treatment and are otherwise resistant. They don't believe that they can be helped and often go undetected. The good news is that many do communicate their intent to die, the large majority are ambivalent about death, and effective treatments do exist."

MILITARY SUICIDE—A NATIONAL CRISIS

Despite the new programs and new staff that the military and VA put in place in the years after Jeff's death, they initially seemed to be chasing a moving target and falling further behind. Wave after wave of returning Americans overwhelmed the system, especially as the Iraq War morphed into a grinding sectarian conflict of suicide bombs and IEDs, followed by the "surge" of additional U.S. forces in Iraq, and then a new surge in Afghanistan. By the time President Obama gave his 2014 State of the Union address, the wounded veteran he praised in the gallery was a young man who had been blown up in Afghanistan on his *tenth* deployment, a number that is difficult to grasp. The long duration of these wars, the multiple deployments, the brutal and unpredictable nature of attacks, and the dwindling public support for the wars, all acted as significant suicide risk factors on a larger scale.

Jeff Lucey's death was the tip of an iceberg. At the time, Jeff's was one of the first reported suicides by a veteran of the Iraq War. Less than a decade later, as the VA and military scrambled to put programs in place, military suicides were widely viewed as epidemic. Paul Rieckhoff of Iraq and Afghanistan Veterans of America put it bluntly in 2007: "The VA system is not at all prepared. This country has not ramped up resources to meet this flood of people coming home."[38] The shocking stories of military suicides pierced denial and highlighted common themes—postwar trauma, difficulties choosing to seek or finding effective help, pained loved ones left in the wake. The Luceys took note of suicides in the news, and because of their visibility and growing connections, they received phone calls from parents and loved ones of suicide victims.

By 2009, with both returning vets and active-duty troops (including those deployed in war zones) killing themselves, the Army vice chief of staff took on the issue as a central mission. He was Peter Chiarelli, and he worked as hard as anyone in the military to address the problems of mental health, PTSD, and suicide. He came to the task from having commanded all U.S. ground forces in Iraq during a rough period there and from having lost 169 soldiers in his own division during his first Iraq deployment. He also deeply regretted that when a memorial to them was built at Fort Hood, Texas, he had agreed to leave off the list a soldier who had committed suicide in Iraq—much as this sensitive issue has led to Jeff Lucey's being left off the Belchertown memorial.

Chiarelli commissioned a study of military suicides.[39] He began convening a monthly meeting of commanders worldwide to go over every case of suicide that month, trying to get to the causes, to identify the stressors and risk factors, and to impress upon the commanders the importance of prevention.[40] He worked with scientists to try to push forward research on the connections with TBI and mental health factors. The Army established the Wounded Warrior Program—in which about half the participants have PTSD, others suffer from physical wounds—to help with transition to civilian life. It set up Warrior Transition Battalions in which active-duty soldiers could remain in the Army while healing wounds, including psychological ones. In 2010, some 200,000 soldiers received mental-health counseling of some form.[41] The military and VA put in place a twenty-four-hour free, confidential suicide prevention hotline for veterans and their loved ones whether enrolled in VA services or not.[42]

Yet, all these efforts continue to swim upstream against the stretched resources of a military at war for too long, against the long-standing culture of stigma around weakness, and against the sheer numbers of service members exposed to the grim realities of Iraq and Afghanistan.[43]

And lest we think that the military stigma around psychological weakness has died out, consider this spoof form that a newly arrived sergeant posted on the wall of his cubicle at a Warrior Transition Battalion a couple of years ago:

> *Hurt Feelings Report. Whiner's Name: . . . Reason for filing this report. Mark all that apply: I am a wimp. I am a crybaby. I want my mommy. I was told that I am not a hero. . . . We, as the Army, take hurt feelings seriously. . . . If you are in need of supplemental*

support, upon written request, we will make every reasonable effort to provide you with a 'blankey,' a 'binky,' and/or a bottle if you so desire. [44]

Furthermore, the trainings, the follow-ups with vets, the flags on medical records all are important advances, but people will fall through the cracks if money and personnel are not there to back them up. As recently as 2012, Army helicopter pilot Ian Morrison called the Pentagon's crisis hotline on his wife's urging. It was his sixth effort in three days to get help for depression. He was put on hold for forty-five minutes. After sending his wife a last text message, "STILL on hold," he shot himself in the family bedroom.[45] Another clue that more must be done.

GETTING VETS INTO TREATMENT

There are four major requirements for a veteran getting professional help: 1) having effective services accessible, 2) identifying problems, 3) believing that help can actually help, and 4) and overcoming resistance to seeking help.

Services now exist. Currently, mental health services are offered to veterans at about 150 VAMCs, 250 Vet Centers, and nearly 800 community-based outreach clinics throughout the United States. Military personnel can access mental health services on most bases. And health insurance carried by active-duty personnel or civilian veterans usually pays for mental health services from private therapists.

There are increasing numbers of civilian mental health workers, including psychotherapists like myself, trained in working with veterans. Still, there is an ongoing need for more civilian psychotherapists to make a commitment to veterans and get the training necessary to be effective. While some veterans prefer to seek out staff at a VAMC or Vet Center because of their experience helping veterans, others distrust the VA system for various reasons and prefer the privacy of a community-based therapist. Many community clinicians are highly trained in working with trauma yet haven't adequately extended their services to veterans. For therapists to serve veterans with professional integrity, it is important that they get fundamental information about military culture, war-related PTSD, and its impact on families.

We have also made progress on understanding the importance of getting help. Many military leaders now implore veterans to find the courage to seek help. As a Marine campaign to reduce mental health stigma states proudly, when Marines encounter a problem, they face it and do what's necessary to prevail.

But it's not just fears of weakness and stigma that get in the way. Many believe that getting help will make things worse. Veterans who have worked hard to avoid reminders of trauma may fear that digging up these issues again will invite trouble. Veterans may have had negative experiences in seeking help in the past. Revealing their stories may have led to bad consequences, such as feeling misunderstood, devalued, judged, or ignored. Some veterans are afraid to reveal what they did during the war for fear of legal consequences. This may have been true for Jeff. Many veterans have come to distrust the system or others in positions of authority. Edgy and irritable veterans may have alienated people in the past and expect that pattern to continue. Veterans who have been pressured into getting services may feel trapped or resentful. Sadly, there are many internal barriers for veterans to avoid treatment, and thus they need persistent encouragement.

Overcoming resistance to seeking help, then, means more than just showing up for appointments. Ultimately, effective psychotherapy requires a sincere commitment to the treatment, and the therapy plan needs to have concrete and realistic goals that the client cares about. Clients should understand that recovery may take time, that the work proceeds in phases, and that they may experience occasional setbacks on the way to full recovery. Effectively addressing military mental health challenges, in my view, will require more than the availability of services and education about their importance. It calls for deeper changes in the culture of military service and in the relationship of civilian society with the military—an issue I will address in the last chapter of the book.

In the end, it is easy to find fault with the federal system charged with caring for war veterans. To their credit, however, the VA and

Department of Defense, carrying the pressure of high expectations and an enormous responsibility, have developed excellent guidelines for clinical intervention. The guidelines outline criteria and strategies for clinical assessment, research-supported treatment techniques, and decision trees to address triage and steps for intervention.[46] The reforms that followed Jeff's death, the suicide prevention efforts, and the persistent campaigns to reduce stigma around mental health needs, all give some hope that the system, in its sluggish way, is moving in the right direction.

chapter 8
BRAIN FREEZE—
UNDERSTANDING PTSD

AS THE LUCEYS advocated for reform and more effective suicide prevention, I was seeing more veterans coming back from war in my therapy practice. What had been a rarity for me and other community-based therapists when the first veterans returned in 2004 was now becoming all too common. I had understood the nature of PTSD before, but I developed a better grasp of how it operates with war experiences in particular.

UNDERSTANDING PTSD

The widely used diagnostic manual known as the DSM-5[47] defines PTSD as a set of symptoms resulting from a traumatic experience of "death, threatened death, actual or threatened serious injury, or actual or threatened sexual violence." Such experiences happen to many service members in wars, as they did to Jeff, but only some develop PTSD afterward, while others never do. It's hard to predict who will and won't, so the symptoms indicate to me as a therapist if the diagnosis of PTSD is appropriate.

The DSM-5 lists four clusters of PTSD symptoms: "alterations in arousal and reactivity, intrusion, avoidance, and negative alterations in cognitions and mood." To see how these manifest themselves, let's consider the story of a veteran I worked with who I'll call "Mike."

Mike came from a military family and had followed suit and joined the Marines. In Iraq, he was a turret gunner, operating a machine gun from the top of a Humvee that accompanied truck convoys. His was usually the last vehicle in the convoy. He deployed at a time, later in the war, when the military put a premium on avoiding civilian casualties, so he operated under rules of engagement that prohibited him from firing his weapon except in clear self-defense when attacked. When he saw threats, he faced a dilemma: responding with too much force would bring his commanders down on him, while too little force could lead to his own death or injury and that of his fellow Marines. He told me in one session, "So [danger] could be comin' toward me and at that point I was like, I'm damned if I do, damned if I don't. . . . We were told that anyone videotaping us was a threat. They were taping a convoy and getting game film. . . . I'm the last truck on that video so he can pretty much pinpoint who is the last truck [and easiest to attack] . . . I know I could have taken them down." But he wasn't allowed to. "The month after I left, a large van blew up a checkpoint, killed two Marines, blew the thing to smithereens." Mike told me that every day he "dealt with the threat of either bodily harm from the enemy or legal harm from the government."

HYPERAROUSAL AND REACTIVITY

What Mike needed in Iraq to succeed, and possibly to survive at all, is what we clinicians call *hypervigilance*. Like many service members, he spent every day scanning his surroundings for potential trouble, for anything that didn't look right. The trouble was that when he came back home, he brought this hypervigilance with him. The first time he came into my office, I noticed that he sat on the edge of his chair leaning forward, his eyes darting around the room. He told me about going with his girlfriend to the Boston Common, a large city park that most people find peaceful and relaxing, but he couldn't enjoy himself as he found himself scanning the rooftops to check for snipers. Many war veterans perceive danger in ordinary public settings back home, such as a shopping mall. They note every detail and every person in case of trouble. My clients who are veterans are usually the most alert to anything that has changed in my office since their last visit. Though this is a normal result of their training, in excess, it may be a sign of PTSD.

Hypervigilance is a form of *hyperarousal*, the keyed-up state of high stimulation that many veterans with PTSD can't turn off. Other variations in this symptom cluster include "irritable or aggressive behavior; self-destructive or reckless behavior; exaggerated startle response; problems in concentration; and sleep disturbance." Veterans may jump, flinch, or tense up, unconsciously reach for weapons, and be suspicious of others, though any of these "reactivity" symptoms can occur individually in moderation in the absence of PTSD as well.

Once, another veteran client of mine was working through a symptom checklist, responding "extremely true" for symptoms including "super alertness or watchful and on guard" and "jumpy or easily startled." Without knowing it, he confirmed his report when he jerked forward in his seat and turned his head toward the sound of a hallway door closing that I had barely noticed.

Sleep disturbance is a common difficulty for veterans and nearly universal for those with PTSD. They often find it hard to turn off the hyperarousal and relax, even when exhausted ("wired tired"), and, as they try to relax, troubling memories may pop up. Sleep difficulties can include difficulty falling asleep or staying asleep, or waking early. Restless sleeping can include violent thrashing and "battle dreams" and can even be dangerous for a bed partner. Nightmares, night terrors, and night sweats are common symptoms of PTSD.

Anger and irritability may show up as impatience, low frustration tolerance, or hostile and cynical attitudes. Some veterans I've known carry chips on their shoulders, resent those perceived as exerting authority over them, and seem to be looking for reasons to be pissed off. My client Mike told me, "I wanna try to avoid any kind of real trouble with like, the law. I don't wanna have to deal with any of that stuff but I can't really let go of my eagerness to mix it up with somebody." He found himself repeatedly "just goin' at it with somebody."

PTSD may fuel people to break things, punch walls, or hurt themselves or others, as when Jeff Lucey punched his bureau.

In the heat of the moment, anger brings on major physiological changes. It releases stress hormones, increases heart rate and blood pressure, heightens sensory perceptions, and tightens muscles in preparation for action. These bodily changes will eventually reverse as the emotion subsides but generally not for at least twenty minutes. Because these bodily processes take over when someone gets angry, I try to help clients make plans to anticipate and de-escalate these reactions before they get out of control.

INTRUSIONS

Another cluster of PTSD symptoms revolves around the intrusion of unwanted thoughts, images, sensory experiences, impulses, memories, and feelings that a person can't seem to get rid of. As the DSM-5 puts it, "the traumatic event is persistently re-experienced . . . [through] recurrent, involuntary, and intrusive memories; traumatic nightmares; dissociative reactions (e.g., flashbacks) . . ." When talking about war experiences, Mike would switch back and forth from past to present tense, a subtle indicator of the past's intrusion into the present. "When I *was* in Iraq," he once told me, "I *am standing* by my truck and my commander *orders* me to . . ." He switched from talking about the memory to talking within it, living in *trauma time* as some therapists call it.[48] Jeff thought he saw camel spiders. One Iraq vet told me that she wakes up eight to ten times a night, drenched in sweat from nightmares. "I'll wake up and, holy shit, I was just back there."

During sleep, intrusions can include dreams that vividly replay a traumatic event, single horrific memories, or more abstract nightmares. The memories may include small fragments of the traumatic experience, or they may mix up elements of the event, but the emotional theme often is consistent. The traumatic experience may be what the veteran most wants to avoid, but the intense and undigested emotion clamors to be resolved. The veteran's mind may have tried to send the memories out of the room, but they keep banging insistently on the door of awareness. When someone is trying to sleep, and is not distracted by daily activity, the banging gets louder, and the door may eventually open.

During the day, flashbacks may similarly intrude with vivid details of a past experience or simply fragments of memory. Flashbacks can also intrude without the person's being aware it is happening. Sometimes intrusions come not as a story with details of the event but in purely bodily and emotional activation. Someone who was in a good mood may suddenly become distracted, irritable, and anxious. An intrusive memory fragment has hijacked his or her good mood, and the person doesn't even understand what happened.

Often, in therapy, the veteran learns to identify the triggers for intrusive memories. A trigger is a circumstance or stimulus that produces a reactive response, usually one that is exaggerated or completely inappropriate to the situation though understandable from the perspective of the past experience that has been triggered. Triggers may be external, such as a loud noise, or internal, such as feeling overwhelmed by daily tasks. These memories may also come up when a person is simply "at ease," including before and during sleep when the body is relaxed and the mind is undistracted by normal waking activities.

Any trauma survivor is prone to having intrusive memories triggered under certain conditions. Memories of events often contain sensory perceptions, thoughts, emotions, and body sensations. A reminder of any one of these components can activate a trauma memory. On good days, the trauma survivor may be able to manage triggers with greater ease—that is, seeing them for what they are and keeping responses under control. But on other days, he or she may be more reactive, such as when fatigued, emotionally distraught, under the influence of alcohol or other substances, or immersed consciously or unconsciously in traumatic memories.

While each individual has unique triggers, there are also common trigger clusters for many veterans. These include direct references to war, including news, movies, and being asked about war experiences when unprepared; bad news, such as a report of a death; loud noises, such as car doors, helicopters, heavy equipment, fireworks, and popcorn popping; smells associated with blood or fuel; driving under hot and dusty conditions, over potholes, or seeing bags by the side of the road; busy highways, overpasses, and even riding in the back seat; and crowded places such as restaurants and shopping malls. Being startled by Middle Eastern or South Asian-looking people, or hearing Arabic spoken, can be, sadly, a trigger for vets who served in Iraq and Afghanistan. Even positive circumstances can sometimes trigger a negative response. For instance, enjoying one's children can activate unresolved guilt for someone who has seen children die in war.

AVOIDANCE

The avoidance cluster refers to the persistent effort to avoid things that stimulate trauma memories, be they "people, places, conversations, activities, objects, or situations" (DSM-5).[49] After multiple bad experiences, Mike avoided social situations where people might irritate him, such as bars because he might get into fights, and kept his distance from other students at his university. Problematically, many people with PTSD avoid therapy. Denial of a problem is a form of avoidance.

Avoidance can ultimately lead to a strong urge to isolate, and this is often enforced by intense feelings of guilt or shame. Thus, relationship problems and social phobias often accompany PTSD. Like other symptoms of PTSD, isolation perpetuates itself, since a person with PTSD will likely feel unworthy and avoid people who might be able to help. This can be quite difficult for veterans' loved ones and care-givers who see them suffering and want to be there for them. But as a Vet Center clinician put it, "Veterans tend to bunker in." Psychiatrist Judith Herman advocates group therapy to help overcome trauma-induced isolation.[50]

Psychological numbing also falls in the avoidance category. One veteran I worked with had become increasingly disinterested in leaving home. He was self-conscious and easily overwhelmed. He likened his feelings to an acid trip he had taken as a teenager. "I feel like I'm on a 'permatrip,'" he said. "Sometimes I don't feel real." This dissociation from reality helped him keep a mental distance from the traumatic memories.

Substance abuse warrants special mention on the list of avoidance strategies. In one large-scale study of people with PTSD, just over half of men and a quarter of women abused alcohol. Marijuana is another commonly overused drug. The understandable impulse to dull the pain leads to alcohol and other drugs, as it did for Jeff Lucey. Dr. Meredith McCarran, who has worked at the Springfield, Massachusetts, Veteran's Center, notes that "alcohol is everywhere in military culture. . . . Between 2:00 AM and 4:00 AM, hotline calls increase. Nobody calls between 7:00 PM and 9:00 PM because everyone is drinking. Whatever someone says they drink, triple it."

NEGATIVE COGNITION AND MOOD

Avoidance and numbing tendencies can shut down emotions, thereby setting up the symptom cluster in which negative thoughts and dark moods take over. A person may show coldness and detachment, a leave-me-alone attitude, intense sadness, and depression, and an inability to have fun. Formerly pleasurable activities, favorite places, and beloved people lose their meaning. Thoughts of suicide may follow. The DSM-5 includes, in this symptom cluster, amnesia about the trauma, persistent negative beliefs about oneself or the world ("I am bad" or "the world is dangerous"), blaming oneself for the traumatic event, and the inability to feel positive emotions.

Mike, for example, became more and more depressed until he lost his ambition to finish school and become a state policeman. His self-esteem dropped, and, though a very likable guy, he was convinced that other people thought badly of him. He felt alienated from other students. Formerly an enthusiastic weightlifter, he stopped going to the gym because he had gained weight after a shoulder injury and thought people would ridicule him as fat. Sitting home instead of going to the gym, he gained even more weight. He felt that civilians didn't understand or respect what he had given for his country. But he was equally bitter toward his commanders. Mike told me, "I swore an oath to defend the Constitution of the United States against all enemies, foreign and domestic, but when I saw my commanding officers putting people at risk, I grew bitter." Wherever he turned, Mike said, he felt like "a square peg in a round hole." Mike's negative thoughts, combined with his avoidant behaviors, intrusive memories, and hyper-arousal, told me that I was dealing with a classic case of PTSD.

TRAUMA AND MEMORY

PTSD symptoms result from the incomplete processing of memories in the brain. Normally, a significant experience leads to a memory that includes feelings, thoughts, sights, and smells. Typically, we turn over the experience in our minds, link it with other relevant experiences, and put whatever is of value into long-term storage where it can later be found and used. When something important happens, people process it consciously by thinking about it or talking about it, but this is just a small slice of the complicated conscious and unconscious processes the brain goes through to make sense of experiences. The brain may dream about the memory during rapid-eye-movement (REM) sleep. Over time, the information is digested and integrated with other memories.

Scientists don't fully understand how the brain stores memories, but thanks to new scanning machines we do know a lot about *where* things happen. For example, we know that an organ in the brain called the hippocampus is associated with working memory and memory storage.

In a nontraumatic experience, such as the time Jeff Lucey went to Disney World and gleefully zapped the costumed characters with his hand buzzer, the memory gets stored away in a digested form after the brain has worked on it, connected it to other experiences, and given it meaning. Years later, Jeff might see a Disney character, or feel a buzzing sensation, or breathe the air of a hot Florida day, and the memory could be triggered in its mature form, shaped by a long-term assessment of what mattered about it and how he felt about it in retrospect after having many other related experiences. Probably the joyful feeling of power from startling a Disney character would be prominent, along with good feelings about his family, while the color of the building he was standing next to would be remembered far less prominently, if at all.

With traumatic experiences, memories do not get stored in this way. The emotional parts of the brain hijack the process, for reasons that make sense in the moment, and normal processing shuts down. The memories get put aside intact. So for instance, when Jeff was driving convoys in Iraq through hostile crowds, feeling bumps in the road but under orders to keep going ("Hit 'em; crush 'em"), his brain did not store that memory normally. The feeling of the bumps. The looks of the people he passed. The smell of diesel fuel. The dust. The noise. All these elements would have been stored away connected within the trauma memory but unprocessed and unintegrated into other knowledge.

Months later, any one of these elements might trigger the entire memory intact. It would be like pushing "play" on his DVD player and having the whole scene replay itself. He would not have figured out what mattered, sorted out the important parts from the rest, or thought through what was his responsibility versus what he had to do under orders. His brain would not have worked out the various associations linked to the diesel smell as experienced on different occasions in his life. The past experience becomes the present reality when the memory is activated and takes over. These are the intrusive memories typical of PTSD.

The reason that traumatic experiences hijack normal memory formation is that the emotional parts of the brain take over in terrifying situations, and the logical thinking parts shut down. I like to explain to clients the "triune brain" model developed by neuroscientist Paul MacLean.[51] The lower part or *reptilian brain* (brainstem, cerebellum) governs basic life-supporting organ functions and mobility, like breathing and balancing. The middle part or *mammalian brain* (limbic system) involves motivations, emotions, and drives. The top part or *human brain* (cerebral cortex) manages complex thinking operations, including planning, understanding actions and consequences, and making difficult decisions. (This is a highly simplified model, but still useful.)

Traumatic situations activate the middle brain in force. In particular, one organ (the amygdala) responds to danger by activating the body's survival response system. Although military training tries to help service members keep thinking clearly in the face of danger,

the instinctive reaction is not so thoughtful. Giving priority to immediate survival, the amygdala stimulates the release of adrenaline and
stress hormones that raise blood sugar levels, speed up breathing and
heartbeat, and increase blood pressure. Meanwhile, the same process
slows down digestive systems, decreases energy storage, reduces sex
hormones, lowers pain perception, and reduces the flow of blood to
anything that's not a muscle.

In that moment, for Jeff driving the convoy or Mike in the turret
of his Humvee, these changes favor survival. All hands are on deck for
the immediate crisis, and in this altered state people can function even
in the middle of horrific scenes. But the normal processing of memories can be one of the casualties since it's not a priority in the moment.
The brain shuts away much of the disturbing information from a traumatic episode, doesn't take time to process it, and keeps functioning
in adversity without becoming overwhelmed by distressing thoughts
and feelings. I think of this capacity as a kind of circuit-breaker in the
human brain to shut down certain mental and emotional processes in
order to keep others going.

Unfortunately, what works in the short term comes at a cost in the
longer term. Later, often months or even years later, if experiences have
not been processed and integrated, the frozen memories work their
way to the surface as the intrusive symptoms of PTSD. Loud noises,
being in tight spaces, or being overheated, for example, can trigger
a panicky feeling throughout the body. One element of the original
memory can trigger the threat alert system as though the entire original situation were present. I've noticed that my clients with PTSD do
not so much *remember* the past as *relive* it. Trigger one component of
the memory network, and the whole package comes rushing out. At
that point, the past dictates the present.

People with PTSD have most of the information needed for
reprocessing a trauma memory but can't access it consistently. They
often have moments when they realize that they shouldn't think or
feel as they do, but this insight does not automatically help to relieve
the distressing symptoms. Over the long term, untreated PTSD
can become chronic—a personality trait rather than a temporary

psychological state. I've worked with Vietnam veterans whose problems with authority and hypervigilance have gone on for so long that those around them see this as just part of their personalities.

Psychological trauma *is physical*. Brain scans show that the memory-related hippocampus in the brain actually shrinks in people with PTSD but grows again after psychotherapy to resolve the PTSD. It's odd to think of myself as a brain surgeon, but clearly psychological wounds are, in fact, physical, and as a person recovers from PTSD, the brain changes.[52] Society at large, and war veterans themselves, too often believe that the physically visible wounds of war are more real and more important than the psychological wounds. This is a destructive myth. Some people return from war with missing limbs, some with traumatic brain injuries (TBI), and some with altered neural memory networks that produce the symptoms of PTSD. All are war injuries, and all deserve respect and appropriate treatment.

WAR AND TRAUMA

My veteran clients describe battle as an intense, chaotic experience unlike anything in civilian life or anything portrayed in war movies. Every instinct tells a combatant to freeze or flee. Among U.S. Civil War soldiers before a battle, "sometimes this fear was so intense that men would fall to the ground paralyzed with terror, bury their face in the grass, grasp at the earth, and refuse to move." In World War II, two-thirds of wounded U.S. soldiers reported being unable to function effectively in combat because of intense fear.[53]

A woman who served in Vietnam as a nurse once showed me photos of her before and after her tour of duty. Though the photos were taken less than a year apart, she appeared to have aged ten years. Her innocent bright eyes had lost their luster.

The elements of confusion and fear resemble some other traumatic experiences, such as assaults, natural disasters, or plane crashes, but the mandate to kill people raises combat trauma to another level. It requires the negation of moral rules that have been taught since childhood, and becoming an active participant in something horrible, not just a victim of it. What goes for killing enemy combatants goes double for killing civilians, bystanders, or prisoners, whether by accident, negligence, or design. As I mentioned, "moral injury" is Jonathan Shay's description of the effects of such actions on those who take them.

Lt. Col. Dave Grossman, a twenty-four-year veteran of military service, wrote two books about the experience of killing in the context of war. He concludes that human beings do not want to kill other human beings. Only a few individuals, perhaps 2 percent of the total population, actually enjoy killing. The rest are "motivated to fight not by ideology or hate or fear," but rather by four factors when the moment of action arrives: 1) group pressures and processes involving their comrades, 2) respect for and direction from their leaders, 3) concern for their own reputation with both officers and comrades, and 4) an urge to contribute to the success of the group.[54]

Armies try to make killing more acceptable through distancing and desensitization. Special language serves this purpose, as psychologist Jim Goodwin noted after the Vietnam War. At boot camp, American soldiers "learned that the Vietnamese were not to be labeled as people but as 'gooks, dinks, slopes, zipperheads, and slants.' When the veterans finally arrived in the battle zone, it was much easier to kill a 'gook' or 'dink' than another human being. This dehumanization gradually generalized to the whole Vietnam experience. . . . Often, many 'slopes' would get 'zapped' (killed) by a 'Cobra' (gunship), and the 'grunts' would retreat by 'Shithook' (evacuation by a Chinook helicopter); the jungle would be sown by 'Puff the Magic Dragon' (a C-47 gunship with rapid-firing mini-gattling guns)." These euphemisms served to blunt the anguish and horror of war during combat. But the military has not taken full responsibility for deconditioning troops or resensitizing them to civilian life.[55]

WOMEN AND WAR TRAUMA

Most service members are men, but war trauma does not inherently affect men and women differently. As women have integrated into the U.S. military over the years, they have experienced PTSD at similar rates to men, relative to combat exposure. Although they are less likely to have killed people, women have more often served in medical occupations in the military, which have an especially high rate of PTSD. A comprehensive study of Vietnam veterans found that 53 percent of men and 48 percent of women (mostly nurses) had experienced "significant stress-reaction symptoms" at some point, with PTSD predicted by exposure to combat conditions more than by gender.

Harvard psychiatrist Judith Herman compared rape and incest survivors with combat veterans. The first involves mostly women, in private, alone. The second involves mostly men, in large groups, out in the open. Yet she found deep similarities—the frozen memories, intrusive thoughts, isolation, and sense that nobody could ever understand.[56]

In the Iraq and Afghanistan wars, U.S. military women participated in combat as military police (MPs), air and naval forces, and support personnel caught up in fighting in the course of their duties. In Iraq, Army combat units borrowed women, known as "lionesses," from noncombat units to participate in night raids (to search women and reduce Iraqi fears of rape). Meanwhile, the MPs, including women, patrolled the streets in Humvees, shooting machine guns at insurgents from the turret. Leigh Ann Hester, an Army National Guard MP in Iraq, became the first woman to earn the Silver Star for valor in close-quarters combat after helping fight off an ambush on the convoy she was protecting. So women have had plenty of exposure to the trauma of combat in these wars and not just from the medical side.

One veteran named Michelle recently shared her Iraq experiences with me. She had fought as a turret gunner with a ground combat unit that was part of the Air Force (and therefore open to women). Three months into Michelle's first deployment, there was a "huge shift in all of us . . . We were killing innocent people because we could." New troops arriving would be shown graphic videos of "dropping bombs, decapitated bodies, messed-up shit" to desensitize them and enrage them. "Anger is key to what you have to do over there," she told me. "If you don't have it, you die."

One time she had to drive a Humvee, and it crashed during an ambush, causing her TBI. Another time, while guarding a gate at the base, she saw a seven-year-old boy she knew shot dead while walking across the adjacent soccer field. She didn't know if the insurgents or the Americans had done it. "That was my turning point," she said later. After returning, Michelle was "a wreck," having trouble with sleep and alcohol, feeling suicidal at times.

Despite two tours and many horrible experiences, her gender became a barrier to getting compensation and treatment from the VA. They gave her 30 percent disability for PTSD when it would have been 70 percent if she'd been male, because "in my records, it never says I was in combat." And she couldn't get into the thirty-day in-patient PTSD program because the VA wouldn't house her with men (though she'd lived with men in Iraq).[57]

American women faced an additional trauma in these wars—military sexual trauma (MST).[58] They risked sexual assault from the very people on whom they depended for their lives—their officers and comrades. In 2008, the VA screening process diagnosed 21 percent of new female veterans with MST. An earlier study found that 60 percent of assaulted female veterans suffered from PTSD as a result of those attacks. Within a hierarchical, and sometimes secretive military organization, reporting sexual harassment or rape can be a "career killer." The crime may be covered up, and the complaint may result in retribution. It doesn't help that military organizations traditionally amp up a hyper-masculine ethos among male troops.

The VA is scrambling to address women's PTSD treatment. It has operated a residential program in California for women with PTSD (97 percent with MST) since 1992. The program has ten beds and treats about forty-five women per year. Nationally, similar VA programs have 124 beds with a capacity of fewer than 600 women annually, out of a population of nearly two million women veterans, including about 350,000 who served in Iraq or Afghanistan. Do the math.

WAR ZONE TO HOME ZONE

As hard as being in a war zone can be, coming home from war can introduce new stressors, often surprising to the returning veterans who look to home for relief from the horrors of war. As Jeff wrote toward the end of his deployment, "I really just want to get home." But the high expectations of home life may collide with realities such as culture shock, alienation from old activities, ungrateful people *or* a strange "celebrity" status, changes with family and friends, work or school challenges, health issues, financial concerns, loss of access to war buddies, and more. If someone has had traumatic experiences during deployment, which have not been resolved and integrated psychologically, the abrupt transition home can contribute to PTSD.

One way of understanding readjustment is to see the distinct differences between life in the *war zone* and life in the *home zone*. In the war zone, troops function under conditions of acute stress. They must stay focused on the mission, remember their roles, follow commands, and adhere to their military training. To do this they must put aside human and emotional needs. For Jeff, the message from boot camp on was that the strong survive. Little or no training prepared him to cope with vulnerability. "Don't go there" is the message. Kevin Lucey came to believe that military training creates preconditions for PTSD, or the inability to recover from PTSD, by stigmatizing weakness. Emotions are liabilities in combat settings.

Dr. E. C. Hurley, a thirty-three-year veteran as an Army chaplain and psychologist who now runs the Soldier Center in Clarksville, Tennessee, portrays the stresses of war as a continuum. Soldiers train to expect and manage short-term stress that comes with intense situations, which can actually improve performance. Even intense stress, if short-term, can bring out a service member's best, as the adrenaline rush and thrill of action focus attention and create confidence. However, chronic stress leads to burn-out. Ongoing exposure to stresses such as combat, IEDs, heat, sleep deprivation, and multiple deployments creates the psychological equivalent of a weakened immune system, creating fertile conditions for PTSD to develop. Service members may return home from war in this weakened condition, but it may not be visible.

The military and VA have come to recognize that coping skills that work well in the war zone can create problems in the home zone (the domestic home and family setting, friendships, jobs, school, and dealing with the general public). The military has increased training for returning veterans and their loved ones to understand the two very different skill sets required at war and at home.[59]

Aggression is a fitting place to start. In war, the veteran must respond with split-second decisions, often in ambiguous environments. Sometimes the stakes are high and lives are at risk. Aggression, fueled by adrenaline and anger, is often the solution to a problem (such as enemy forces shooting at you). At home, the same aggressive responses can backfire. Some vets may head to bars with good intentions but then the drinking eases their inhibitions, and if someone annoys or offends them in a barroom exchange, matters can heat up quickly and lead to an explosive incident. Others may withdraw socially to avoid the fights they keep getting into. Many struggle with road rage. Woe to the offending driver who forgets to use directional signals or slows down for a yellow light rather than gunning through the intersection. I've known veterans who have changed their route to tail a "bad" driver until they could find a chance to retaliate.

Indeed, driving itself differs drastically in the two zones. To get somewhere safely in a combat zone requires going fast and being unpredictable, changing lanes quickly, straddling the middle line, and staying away from other vehicles that might explode. At home, driving safely means pretty much the opposite—being predictable, staying in your lane, following rules, tolerating other vehicles, and avoiding tickets or accidents.

Another dimension is the *constant alertness* demanded in the war zone. Hypervigilance works for a war zone, as Mike found scanning the road from his turret. Even when resting, a person is ready to move into full action at a moment's notice. At home, however, a veteran needs to relax and find time for pleasures. To always scan for trouble and make mountains out of molehills can unsettle the veteran's relationships. Families and friends soon learn to accommodate the veteran by shrugging off the hit-the-floor reflex whenever there's a loud noise or by letting the veteran be the last one to walk into a room. But these adjustments can increase isolation and friction.

In the war zone veterans went to bed knowing exactly what they would do if suddenly woken. The sleep they got was often "with one eye open," a habit that contributes to the common problem veterans have with sleeping. Unfortunately, many veterans develop problematic strategies for relaxing, such as drinking and other drug use or escaping into activities that serve as an avoidance of their daily responsibilities.

In the war zone, *the mission objective* is paramount, and rules of authority are key to achieving it. At home, rules and roles are more complex. A healthy relationship often involves fluid changes, shared decision-making, and times when it's your call or the other's. Many veterans are excellent employees in jobs that are clear in their expectations and lines of authority but struggle when they are expected to intuitively figure out what to do. One client of mine, surprised by his trouble adjusting to home, said, "I like structure. I like to get shit done. Everybody dillydallies. People start talking and I want them to get to the point. In the military, people are direct."

In the war zone, *response tactics* dictate quick and decisive action, following training and commands from above. At home, especially in the normal chaos of raising young children, the veteran may feel too much going on and want to step in to create order, forcefully if necessary. The veteran may also seek order in how the home is kept, how people dress, or how they act. This need to have things a certain way can come across as selfish, cold, rude, aggressive, and even abusive. Spouses and children may suffer at the bottom of this chain of command. Children didn't enlist in their families, and their developmental needs and capabilities may be poorly met by a parent who expects absolute obedience.

The war zone offers high *stimulation* (interspersed with periods of boredom). Little decisions can be critically important. Back home, choices can seem unimportant. Vets can get itchy for more action. Some may long to return to war. Some turn to high-risk behavior, such as driving fast or picking fights, for an adrenaline rush. Though dangerous, it helps them feel alive. They may develop addictive behaviors in their search for excitement, including gambling, sex, impulsive spending, alcohol, and other drugs. Exercise and engaging activity can meet the need for action, but a keyed-up veteran can still stress others out, and family members can resent the spoiling of their peace and quiet.

Veterans sometimes develop a disdain for the cushy life that Americans lead and for the importance civilians place on things that don't really matter, such as how to dress, what to eat, or which TV shows to follow. When those who have never been to war complain about the heat, bad road conditions, or a bad night's sleep, it can be hard for the veteran to relate. Even most war movies do not ring true. In actual war, gory images do not flash briefly on the screen but remain, and the people, dead and alive, are real.

Handling information follows strict rules in the war zone, where information is a military asset upon which lives depend and that can create strategic advantages or disadvantages. Depending on your rank and role, you are restricted from information or expected to restrict others from it. When denied information, you generally have no recourse. A healthy life in the home zone, however, requires more open sharing of information, communication of feelings, and cooperative problem-solving. Veterans may keep things to themselves. They may be impatient with small talk, and when they do talk, it's all business, serious, and purposeful. This could give their loved ones the wrong impression that the veteran doesn't care about them or want to share home life with them—all the more so when veterans leave the house to seek out old battle buddies who know what's on their minds.

Most sensitive is information about what veterans experienced in the war. Even when civilians are prepared to learn about their experiences, discussed at the right time and place, many veterans remain prickly to an invitation to talk. They may feel shame, may not be able to translate the war experience into terms a civilian could understand, or may not want to burden their loved ones. Jeff, for one, seemed to guard his war zone experiences with great secrecy and was sure nobody could understand them. Family members or friends may eventually give up asking.

The relationship to *weapons* is also completely different in the war and home zones. While deployed, veterans keep their weapons available and ready for use at all times. At home, they may feel naked without their weapons. They may carry weapons illegally, fail to secure a loaded weapon at home, or bring lethal force into a minor conflict. In war, they have been intentionally desensitized to using lethal force. At home, this can land them in jail. "In combat, it's dangerous to be unarmed; at home, it's dangerous to be armed," as the Army has explained it to returning soldiers.[60] Even a baseball bat in the back of the pickup truck or a knife under the front seat, especially when combined with unbridled anger or alcohol, can quickly lead to an alarming escalation.

Emotions must be handled differently in the two zones. At war, emotions like fear, sadness, and anger, which are strongly triggered by the circumstances, need to be put aside in favor of logical decision-making. Once home, veterans often battle between their training to put emotions aside and the surging need to face some of the emotions they packed away while deployed. Some become numb to emotions, though perhaps punctuated by momentary surges of anger, sadness, or intense anxiety. Some find not just fear and grief hard to express but also positive emotions such as love and happiness. That absence can suffocate families. And some veterans can't tolerate other people's emotions—an understandable reaction but another source of friction in the family.

Despite all these difficulties in the transition from war to home, many veterans have a counterbalancing strength—the resilience they have developed in tough conditions. The veteran can come back stronger, wiser, and more compassionate. War experiences can build confidence, perspective, and overall maturity. The negative effects can diminish or be transformed, given some time, support, and professional services when needed.

A danger inherent in the increasing emphasis in American society on addressing veterans' mental health challenges is the mistaken impression that vets are generally damaged, fragile, or prone to falling apart. The reality is that 80 percent do not have PTSD, the great majority have not been wounded, and although war may not have been a positive experience, it may nonetheless have left them stronger and more resilient. Americans need to know that if you hire a vet—or marry a vet—the odds-on likelihood is that you are getting someone tested and proven in hard conditions, with great maturity and leadership ability for his or her age.[61]

RELATED PROBLEMS

As veterans with PTSD adapt to the home zone, they often face related mental health issues that partially overlap and make life more difficult. In one large-scale study, 88 percent of men and 79 percent of women with PTSD met criteria for another psychiatric or behavioral disorder. The most common were major depression (48 percent of men, 49 percent of women), alcohol abuse (52 percent of men, 28 percent of women), conduct disorders (43 percent of men), drug abuse (35 percent of men), phobias (29 percent of women), and social phobias (28 percent of women).

Therapists often measure depression using tools like the Beck Depression Inventory, which is a series of straightforward questions that takes about twenty minutes to complete. And when a person is depressed, there should automatically be an assessment of suicidality.[62]

One indicator of depression is decreased sexual interest. Traumatized war veterans have often suffered from sexual problems, famously discussed in the British literature on men who had fought in World War I. This makes sense in the context of stress hormones' effect of shutting down reproductive hormones. Survival comes first, reproduction later. The front line of combat is a sexless place (in contrast to rear bases).[63] Veterans who suffer from PTSD are still, in a sense, in battle, and they are still primed for survival more than sex.

Survivor guilt is another depression-related symptom for war veterans. War creates death and casualties. Many war veterans have seen death, and some have faced multiple losses, including close buddies—the people they are most bonded to. A veteran may ask, "Why did I survive and not them?" A person may feel guilt for what he or she did or didn't do, and these thoughts tend to resist logical explanations. Superstitious thinking even comes up as veterans look for a sense of control: "My friend was killed because I let him show me a picture of his girlfriend." There is little time to grieve in the war zone, and unresolved grief may emerge later on. Some veterans carry guilt from a "high" they felt from killing. "I did something I can't talk about" may be code for guilt trauma.

Trauma-related symptoms often play out as physical ailments. It has been said that in response to trauma, "the body keeps the score."[64] PTSD, even if consciously denied, manifests itself as headaches, gastrointestinal complaints, immune system problems, dizziness, chest pain, and other bodily ailments. PTSD often amplifies physical pain, and chronic pain afflicts many veterans who suffered wounds and injuries. Tinnitus, constant ringing in the ears, affects veterans exposed to explosions and other noise.

The risk of domestic violence in the families of returning veterans is significant. One pre-Iraq study based on interviews of veterans with PTSD and their partners revealed that 42 percent of the men had engaged in physical aggression against their partners in the previous year, 92 percent had been verbally aggressive, and 100 percent had used psychological aggression (based on combined veteran/partner reports of violence).[65]

Veterans overall had much higher violence rates than nonveterans—six times higher for all violence and fourteen times higher for severe violence—and rates for vets with PTSD were somewhat higher still. Behind this violence typically lies anger combined with emotional numbness, social withdrawal, negative self-view, fear of abandonment, and, of course, alcohol use.

Traumatic brain injury (TBI) is another signature injury of the Iraq and Afghanistan wars, mostly because of IEDs and suicide bombings. Depending on the location and severity of the injury, cognitive processes can be impaired for short- or long-term periods. Many symptoms resemble PTSD or depression, sometimes leaving one or the other condition undiagnosed or minimized.

RESERVISTS

Many common threads connect the war-to-home experiences of service members in different branches and components. However, reservists and National Guard members face particularly challenging transitions.

Active-duty service members generally return to a base. Although they may now live with family on or near base, they are still in uniform every day. Their families will have had access to many community resources, especially the other families nearby, during the deployment. People around the base "get" what's going on, and the base probably has mental health and health care services. On the other hand, the job comes with frequent relocations, requiring the family to start all over again in new areas—with new schools, new friends, new dentists, new everything—which can be isolating.

In contrast, reservists and Guard members—"citizen soldiers" like Jeff—are rarely in uniform after their deployment. They may see their unit only one weekend a month and two weeks each summer. They have, or at least had, a civilian job. Although reservists' families don't have to move repeatedly, they rarely live near a base, and veteran-friendly community resources are harder to find. These families are in the minority in their communities and may feel invisible, different, and misunderstood.

SUPPORTING FAMILIES

Secondary traumatization is a risk that comes with witnessing and having to deal with a loved one with PTSD. As much as Jeff's PTSD was the focus of attention, his parents, sisters, and girlfriend were traumatized by his PTSD as well, both before and after his suicide.

The main focus of military and VA efforts to address mental health issues has naturally been on the troops returning from war. But the loved ones also need support. They have their own challenges, as society too readily dumps the problem of veterans with adjustment challenges into their laps.

Kevin and Joyce Lucey wrote this about military families:

These are the loved ones and family members who have walked with their soldier right from the very beginning, boot camp. These are the people who extend themselves way beyond to support these troops, . . . stand with them as they leave on deployment; wait for them while dealing with all the various stressors; stand so proudly as their loved one returned, . . . doing all this while dealing with all the stressors existing in their lives—usually with little support.

Then once home, the family may find themselves waging other struggles in a very different kind of a battlefield—trying to help their loved one if not trying to keep them alive. Our families suffer so much pain which is so difficult to describe . . . it can range from sleep deprivation, stress, explosive anger, substance abuse, and guilt to complicated grief for those of us who have lost our service member—the Gold Star Families and families such as ours. As with the wounded, those of us who have survived the loss of our loved one bear our own wounds in all of our lives, which then ripple out impacting many more lives.

I see these families in my therapy practice. I worked with one family in which the father had been in Iraq for several months. The mother was at home working full-time and looking after their two teenagers. She was on the edge every day. She worried daily about her husband and tried to compartmentalize her feelings. She assumed her kids were affected by their father's absence as well, but they wouldn't say so when asked directly. It just seemed to come out in their behavior. There was an extra resistance to every parental request the mother made. Completing homework, getting to the dinner table when the food was hot, simple chores, and doing their part to look after the dog—all things that had gone relatively smoothly in the past—became battles at home for an overtaxed mother who was admittedly resentful about having all the parental responsibility.

At one point, the father flew to his base in North Carolina for a week of reprieve. He wasn't free to come home, so the mother decided to drive the kids down there. They were all excited to see him, but they were in such a state of tension that they argued about little things all the way down. At one point the mother had had enough backtalk from her daughter in the passenger seat. Impulsively, she backhanded her daughter in the face. They were all stunned, and the car turned silent. It was an ugly incident that would lead to apologies on both sides, and ultimately they were able to admit how much the father's absence affected them.

In another family, "Ron" had deployed into combat and his unit suffered extensive casualties. There were many moments in which he thought he would never return home. He had voluntarily chosen this deployment because it paid well and would financially benefit his family, but he was worn down by the end of the mission. He longed to return home. But he returned to a family in chaos. When he entered his home for the first time, it was a mess. His two young sons hid from him. His wife was at her wit's end. She said that the children were out of control, and she resented that everything had been on her shoulders. Now she wanted Ron to come in and straighten the situation out.

Ron's return shook up the family authority structure, and the oldest son resented the father's power. Ron was glad to be back with his kids, but he was used to a command system in which adherence to his directives was a life-and-death matter. It was hard for him to give any slack when his family resisted his attempts to restore order or his son challenged his authority. Ron worked hard to transcend his own disappointment and resentment of the home-zone challenges and to understand what his family had gone through without him.

These challenges exist across the country, Within the Army, Air Force, Marines, Navy, and Coast Guard, there are 1.4 million individuals on active duty. Half of these have spouses, and there are more than a million children of active-duty personnel. The National Guard and Reserve add another million service members, half a million spouses, and 700,000 children. Millions more veterans who served in Iraq and Afghanistan but are retired from the military account for millions more spouses and children. Add to that millions of siblings, millions of extended family members, and millions of close friends. The scale is massive.

For the spouse and co-parent left at home, coping with the extra effort is wearing and, especially if the other parent is unable to give emotional support, can lead to burnout and resentment.[66] Being overwhelmed by the difficulty of the job as a parent can easily lead to resentment of the deployed partner and indirectly toward the children themselves. As strong as their love may have been, couples can become estranged as time passes during deployment. The partner at home has needs for companionship and intimacy that sometimes lead to betraying the marriage commitment. Affairs can happen on both sides of the ocean.

All the strains during deployment can build up yet are kept in check by the demands of the moment and the expectation that everything will be great once the deployment is over. Yet that is when the built-up pressures can explode. Research suggests that those at greatest risk for post-deployment adjustment difficulties are young and recently married couples, lower-ranking service member families, younger children, and families that were not functioning well before deployment.[67]

Largely hidden in the wave of military suicides in recent years is a secondary wave—suicides among family members. When families suffer war-related losses and troubles, it is hard to move on. A recent CNN special, *The Uncounted*, captures the emerging stories and statistics of family members and other loved ones who have battled their own suicidal thoughts.[68] The loyal and largely silent family members remain almost invisible in the wake of our recent wars, and nobody has counted how many have developed PTSD or killed themselves during the stresses of deployment and post-deployment.

To the positive, military families tend to be close-knit and supportive. Family members deployed can create and deepen the bonds of a family as it unites as a team. Military families link up to form communities within a community. Strong core values for military families include patriotism, duty, honor, and courage. Of course, military families are diverse, and each one is unique. For therapists, it is important to understand and respect the culture, traditions, and values of military families, and to learn about the conditions they may face, but not to make assumptions.

CHILDREN

Children are especially vulnerable to secondary trauma when a parent has PTSD. While one adverse event will not derail healthy development, accumulating stressful incidents may compromise the child's ability to adapt. Factors that may increase or decrease the child's ability to cope include his or her individual temperament, the nature of family relationships, the availability of an emotionally attuned caregiver, and the influence of the larger community. Children's understanding of why their veteran parents are having trouble, and the meaning they associate with it, are significant. With support, they can better understand why the veteran parent isn't the same all the time. The child's own reactions can be validated, and he or she can learn ways to adjust without taking the blame for the stress.

Research shows that when a spouse is deployed, the other spouse has, on average, more symptoms of depression and increased stress, and there is less family cohesion and structure. During deployment, rates of child mistreatment and neglect nearly double, and both children and adolescents have more behavior problems. With the return of the absent parent, the research shows a direct relationship between the veteran's PTSD symptoms and the impact on children.[69]

These children may respond in three potentially problematic ways: 1) the overidentified child experiences secondary traumatization and comes to experience many of the symptoms of the parent with PTSD, 2) the rescuer child takes on parental roles and responsibilities to compensate for the parent's difficulties, and 3) the emotionally uninvolved child receives little emotional support, which results in problems at school, depression and anxiety, and relational problems later in life.[70]

Too little or too much sharing with children can be problematic. Silence can leave the child unable to discuss the obvious changes in a parent who has been to war, and the child may bottle up feelings. However, overdisclosure by parents, such as the sharing of graphic details from traumatic incidents, can leave impressions seared in the child's mind.[71]

The term *ambiguous loss* refers to the sense that someone is there but not there during deployment. When the veteran returns, children often expect and need more. They crave a return to the best of what they had. When this doesn't happen, it is often deflating and confusing. For the family in which the veteran withdraws into the clutches of PTSD, the ambiguous loss continues.[72]

REUNIONS

As America's wars end, there will be far fewer reunions of returning troops with their families. This is fortunate because the time of reunion can be surprisingly hard on families. One might expect that separation, as the service person heads into the dangers of war and the unknown, would be more difficult than returning to the love and security of the known. Yet, a host of challenges come with the attention that the returning veteran receives. The brave face of the proud and victorious warrior, put on for the benefit of the home crowd, may hide an inner warrior who feels tired and wounded, even broken.[73]

Similarly, most family members, as they launch their service members off to war, typically show their best faces—their love, their pride in his or her commitment, and their hope and faith that the person will be OK and home soon. Beneath the surface, family members often feel apprehension or full-scale fear about the fate that awaits the service member as well as the challenges looming on the home front. The brave faces at the time of goodbyes, however, need to be maintained for only a short time, and then both sides get down to the work of coping with their fate while apart.

At the reunion, however, the brave faces lead into a long period of togetherness in which underlying issues are bound to come out. Furthermore, during the goodbyes and while the deployment continues, both sides often comfort themselves with an idealized homecoming imagined in the future. When that day actually arrives, it would be hard to meet these idealized expectations. A common fantasy is that if the veteran just makes it back safely, everything will be just the same as when the veteran left. But of course people have continued to change, and everything is not the same as before, even without PTSD or other wounds.

Family life after war *can* be good, it can be sweet, a couple can appreciate each other more having faced the difficulties of being apart. But parents, spouses, partners, and children of returning veterans all need support—much more support than society gives them today. Kevin and Joyce Lucey ran a support group for families, knowing what they were going through. And the military and VA are stepping up programs to support families as well. But collectively our efforts still fall short of the need.

The Jeff Luceys of our world served and paid a terrible price. But so did the Kevins, Joyces, Debbies, Kellys, Julies, and the rest. Not only is it wrong for the society to overtax a small segment to fight our wars, but it's doubly wrong to put the burden of cleaning up afterward on the families, parents, and children, most of whom never enlisted for the job, weren't trained for it, and don't get paid. We should be saying to the spouses, parents, children, and friends of those who've fought our wars, "Thank *you* for your service."

chapter 9
FULL RECOVERY—TREATING PTSD

IN 2012, A young man I'll call "Ben" came into my office to get help with his PTSD. He had joined the Army and become a Ranger, the elite group whose creed calls for its members to arrive "at the cutting edge of battle by land, sea, or air . . . [and] move further, faster, and fight harder than any other soldier," and show mental, physical, and moral strength, gallantry, and "intestinal fortitude." Ben was a medic, so he saw plenty of blood during tours in Iraq and Afghanistan, where he had deployed to the most dangerous part of the country, the Korengal Valley, site of the documentary *Restrepo*. He had been blown up in trucks on four occasions.

Ben had returned home and enrolled at a university, he told me, but then had shut down, unable to concentrate and feeling alienated from the other college students who were younger and clueless about war. He didn't seek out other veterans on campus; they just reminded him of what he wanted to forget. He was irritable and had angry outbursts over small things, though he was mostly upset with himself, and he wondered if he had much to offer the woman he loved, who he was to marry in a few months. He had trouble falling asleep, sometimes had intrusive flashbacks (though at other times the war seemed surreal as though it had never happened), and was troubled by suicidal thoughts, although he had no intention of acting on them. His fiancée pressed him to get help, and he was referred to me by his doctor. Ben knew he had PTSD and was highly motivated to do whatever he could to improve his state of mind. Before I describe the highlights of Ben's therapy in detail, let me explain in general terms how I approach treatment for PTSD.

PHASES OF TREATMENT

PTSD *can* be treated. In fact, with the right treatment, reduction of major PTSD symptoms can occur more quickly than generally expected. The goal of recovery as I view it is not to erase memories or to deny war experiences. Instead, it is to face and transform these memories in a way that ultimately reduces or eliminates the emotional disturbance linked to these experiences. Beyond that, full recovery means reaching a realization that the traumatic experience is truly over and that one not only survived but learned from what happened.

PTSD trauma recovery has three phases. First, *stabilization* involves identifying the problems, reducing the most acute symptoms, and building motivation and commitment to the recovery process. Once someone is stable enough to proceed to the second phase, *trauma treatment* involves more directly facing and working through specific traumatic memories. The third phase, *integration*, is aimed at repairing the indirect effects of PTSD, including the impact on relationships, health, opportunities in the world, self-regard, and blocks to personal fulfillment. Working through grief, not only for lost comrades but for the costs of PTSD to oneself, is an important component of integration work. The veteran can now focus energy into building the life he or she wants to have rather than just coping. Those veterans who have been able to do the hard work of full recovery complete a journey from surviving to thriving.

STABILIZATION

The stabilization phase sets the stage for treatment success. Ben came in motivated and focused on getting better. He was ready to grapple with his problems. By contrast, Jeff came to see me in an acute state of crisis, after a long downward spiral struggling with personal problems. He could not make rational decisions if he wanted to. Certainly, he was not ready to unpack whatever traumatic memories lurked within him. Sadly, he was in the grip of the trauma without enough perspective to see it as a problem he could fix.

Stabilization for Jeff seemed to require a secure twenty-four-hour environment until he could feel safe enough on his own and could buy into a plan for his own recovery. For others who are not in such a state of desperation, stabilization may mean addressing day-to-day struggles such as substance abuse, life management problems, troubled relationships, and other immediate problems. Many vets scramble to find jobs, make ends meet financially, or in some cases, even maintain a home. Finding solutions to these issues is an integral part of mental health support.

During the stabilization phase, veterans are taught to build the capacity to observe what they are going through in a somewhat detached way, so they aren't consumed and defined by their traumatic memories, and so that they have psychological leverage to outmaneuver these forces. They learn to identify their personal strengths and skills as part of their healthier identity. They may need help remembering a time when their lives were not dominated by their problems. Many people with PTSD function adequately much of the time, but they do need help anticipating and coping with triggers.

Another key element of phase-one trauma work involves creating a strong and secure relationship of trust with treatment providers, whether an individual therapist or a treatment system such as the VA. Veterans need to sense that they are fundamentally respected, not only for their service but for who they are as people, in spite of their difficulties. Maintaining personal dignity is paramount.

The chance to tell their stories and be heard respectfully is key. After more than thirty years of experience as a VA therapist, Dr. Susan Rogers learned that "letting the veteran tell their story is critical in the treatment. If the choice is the four-minute version or the four-hour version, I go for the four-hour." She adds, "But you need to help them and keep them from shutting down. If you lose them, they may not come back for years."

At the same time, many people think that working with a caring and compassionate therapist who is empathic and a good listener is enough for therapy to be effective. But research shows that a strong therapeutic alliance, developed in phase one, is of limited value unless it is used as a vehicle for working directly with intense negative emotions in the second phase of treatment.[74] The therapist must have trauma-specific skills and training for successful PTSD treatment along with those basic clinical skills of empathic listening and emotional attunement.

An important advancement in treatment over the last ten years is the realization that the old model of deferring trauma treatment until a person is clean and sober is misguided. The current harm-reduction intervention strategies put priority on treatment for alcohol and drug abuse but concurrently address trauma as a source of intense and ongoing emotional pain.

Stabilization does not require solving all of a person's life issues before starting in on the core trauma treatment. Rather, the goal is for the client to have enough coping strategies so that facing traumatic memories won't make matters worse. Facing traumatic memories will ease most difficulties, but it takes a certain inner strength and stability to do so. Even when phase-two treatment is underway, other common difficulties may require ongoing attention, including depression, stress, sleep disturbance, problematic anger and violence, relationship difficulties, substance abuse, guilt and grief, traumatic brain injury, and suicidality.

For many veterans, a crucial first step is to learn techniques for stress management, such as physical and mental relaxation, positive thinking, exercise, prayer, and problem-solving. Anger-management programs can be helpful for many veterans with PTSD as they simultaneously address the underlying trauma issues. Anger-management techniques include learning to take responsibility for one's anger, identifying the warning signs when someone has been triggered toward anger, and having strategies for calming down and distancing from the triggering situation. In cases of ongoing emotional abuse or physical violence, a therapist should make immediate interventions and referrals focused on prioritizing the safety of all involved.

Because sleeplessness exacerbates other difficulties, improving the quality of sleep is a high treatment priority. Veterans can learn strategies to improve their sleep by developing healthy routines and practicing self-calming methods. Unhealthy strategies like drinking need to be discouraged, as drinking alcohol to calm down ultimately impairs the sleep process. Some veterans find that they can sleep better during the daytime when it may feel safer, although this reversed pattern can be isolating and disruptive to other life activities.

Facing loss and profound sadness is often an ongoing journey for veterans, who may need permission and support to move through complex feelings of anger, guilt, and sadness about losses. Veterans may need to make time to talk and grieve with other veterans. Unprocessed grief often leads to depression. Anniversary dates of tragic war experiences can be powerful triggers. Veterans often benefit from anticipating these days and perhaps planning a symbolic activity to honor the memory. Other ways to process loss can include writing about good memories, regrets, and current feelings, or perhaps even writing a heartfelt letter to the deceased person from the heart. Joyce Lucey, for example, wrote to her son for her own solace. Likewise, creating a symbolic memorial or photo album can also help document and honor loss and free a grieving person to move on in life.

Many grieving veterans suffer from survivor guilt, and it can be difficult to pry someone away from a guilty conscience. Sometimes well-timed questions can help someone see that he or she was in a situation with no good options. When a person understands that guilt won't change the past, he or she can grieve and let go of the idea that guilt is somehow useful or honorable. Often, survivors fear harsh judgment or rejection if they reveal their guilt. Sometimes, I ask people to simply imagine sharing their secrets with another person and how that person might actually respond. Often they realize the listener is likely to be more receptive than they had assumed. Learning to forgive oneself is often what is needed.

Sometimes antidepressants or other medications are prescribed to jump-start a depressed psychobiological system. In addition, when trying to break out of depression, it is often easier to change behavior rather than wait to feel better first. But veterans may need repeated encouragement to mobilize the energy to try things that used to be fun or even new activities. Changing certain strategically chosen behaviors, even though a person may not "feel like it," can lead to more positive thoughts, emotions, and general well-being. In cases of chronic physical pain, pain management using medications and other methods can be an important part of stabilization as well. However, the risk of abusing pain medications needs to be monitored.

Ultimately, if coping skills require constantly avoiding bad memories and shutting out feelings or people, they will not be sustainable. Ironically, the trauma is in control of a person's life if he or she is working too hard to avoid it. By contrast, when stress and suffering are better managed, the heavy-duty memories can then be faced and resolved, loosening their grip on daily life.

FOUR TREATMENT APPROACHES

The trauma treatment of stage two aims to eliminate or reduce PTSD symptoms. The 2010 VA/DOD Clinical Practice Guidelines recommend four treatment approaches for PTSD as offering the highest level of benefit.[75] In brief, *exposure-based therapies* (ET) bring up traumatic memories through imagined or acted-out scenarios, or through oral or written stories, while helping the client restructure thoughts (such as actual versus perceived danger) and learn relaxation techniques. (Some therapists recently have experimented with virtual-reality simulators to expose veterans to realistic wartime scenarios during therapy.) *Cognitive-based therapies* (CT) work with clients specifically to change the thoughts and beliefs connected to the traumatic event, though also often including relaxation techniques and general discussion of the event. *Stress inoculation training* (SIT) teaches methods of breathing and muscle relaxation and includes cognitive elements (self-dialogue, thought-stopping, role-playing) and often exposure techniques. *Eye Movement Desensitization and Reprocessing* (EMDR) uses alternating eye-movements combined with an exposure component (recalling the traumatic event), a cognitive component (reassessing thoughts and beliefs), and a self-monitoring of emotion and body reactions component.

These four approaches meet the standards for evidence-based psychotherapies, meaning that research has substantiated their effectiveness for PTSD treatment. Each recognizes that PTSD symptoms include a mixture of cognitive, emotional, physiological, and behavioral symptoms. Each provides structured intervention procedures. The guidelines also recognize benefits from complementary interventions, such as education about PTSD, hypnosis, relaxation techniques, group therapy, family therapy, or medication (among others).

HOW EMDR WORKS

EMDR psychotherapy, my own specialty, was founded by psychologist Francine Shapiro some twenty-five years ago and is based on her Adaptive Information Processing model of trauma. In this model, PTSD symptoms result from information about an experience that is incorrectly processed in the brain. The symptoms can be healed by therapy that allows the brain to reprocess the information correctly.[76] Treatment aims to pinpoint the traumatic memories associated with current difficulties, desensitize them to allow normal memory processing and storage, and transform clients' understanding of themselves and the experiences they have lived through.[77]

While research has found all four treatment approaches effective for PTSD, in my view properly administered EMDR therapy is the most *efficient* treatment for war-related PTSD available today. More than twenty randomized clinical trials have shown its effectiveness, and it is recognized as a top-level trauma treatment in practice guidelines worldwide, including the American Psychiatric Association, the World Health Organization, the International Society for Traumatic Stress Studies, and the National Center for PTSD.

EMDR works quickly and its effects last. One study on EMDR treatment for combat veterans with multiple experiences of traumatic stress reported that twelve treatment sessions resulted in a 77 percent elimination of PTSD.[78] In another study, seventy-two active-duty military personnel, more than half of them diagnosed with combat PTSD, received EMDR treatment by therapists in different clinics. The disturbance level associated with the targeted traumatic memories fell dramatically, a more positive perspective was generated, and symptom scores fell from the severe range to mild or below. These changes occurred in an average treatment time of about eight sessions for wounded veterans and four sessions for those without injuries.[79]

With EMDR, a single-event trauma is normally treated within three to six sessions. More chronic PTSD requires more extensive treatment, but once a person is stabilized, the major symptoms of traumatic memories can typically be greatly reduced within several months. Contrary to Vietnam-era messages to soldiers such as "PTSD is something you just learn to put up with," EMDR has the track record to show that war trauma can be overcome and often in a surprisingly short period of time.

Although I find cognitive-based therapies effective in many aspects of therapeutic work, especially for early stabilization, when it comes to trauma resolution, EMDR more fully heals traumatic memories. Cognitive approaches focus on changing a person's thought patterns, which can reduce the power of traumatic memories to disrupt life in the present. The new thoughts can fortify the person and help him or her manage symptoms and tamp down negative thoughts, feelings, and behavior. But this new layer of thoughts does not actually resolve the underlying frozen traumatic memory. It puts a good face on it, so to speak, often masking symptoms that remain corrosive beneath the surface.

EMDR takes a different approach as the client moves into phase two, which is trauma resolution. The process is based on unpacking the traumatic memory and guiding the client to sort through and repack the experience, allowing the person's own mind to generate adaptive new insights and perspectives. In metaphoric terms, the client's mind unpacks a cluttered closet to reorganize only what is needed and throw out the rest. EMDR fosters the brain's ability to make new connections within the mind by allowing those fragmented memories to link up with other more positive and adaptive knowledge. EMDR elicits the brain's natural tendency toward health and balance, thereby creating the conditions for the client to re-examine an experience, draw different conclusions, and allow rigid and distorted post-trauma beliefs to soften and shift.

The fully reprocessed memories, when activated, no longer produce distressing and disruptive reliving experiences but can be recalled safely without pulling the veteran out of his or her current life and into trauma mode. After successful EMDR treatment, all the main symptoms of PTSD—the intrusions, reactivity, avoidance, negative beliefs, and mood problems—have been addressed. At this point, traumatic memories are more fully integrated and held in a new, more resolved form, generally with little or no remaining emotional pain and with a greater sense of the wisdom gained from having come through a life-altering experience.

With EMDR, the desensitization and reprocessing of traumatic memories takes place in a way that clients tolerate much more readily than other therapeutic approaches, such as Prolonged Exposure (which can require repeated and prolonged retelling of the traumatic experience). EMDR assures clients that they are in control of the level of exposure to the traumatic memories and helps them keep within their own tolerance levels.

In my clinical experience, clients seem to stay with EMDR treatment, tolerate the challenges of working with painful memories, and see more significant benefits sooner than with other treatment methods. EMDR also differs from cognitive approaches in that it requires no structured "homework," partly because the healing process operates on an unconscious level and takes place in the controlled conditions of the therapy office. Yet, EMDR also generally shortens the total amount of time needed for relief from traumatic memories. Consequently, I have found that EMDR treatment is typically more efficient than other treatments, more user-friendly, and has a lower client dropout rate. I also find that therapeutic gains are maintained over time.

THE EMDR PROCESS

EMDR uses a multi-stage approach. First, the client and therapist work together to identify the past experiences that have laid the groundwork for current trauma symptoms, including current triggers. Later, EMDR helps build a more positive mindset to face the future. During treatment, various procedures and protocols guide the therapy.

Before the trauma reprocessing stage, the client learns what to expect and makes a choice whether to proceed. The therapist then guides the client to identify and strategically *target* particular traumatic memories. These memories are chosen based on a number of factors, including the level of disturbance associated with the memory, the time that the client experienced them (oldest memories generally go first), and the degree of relevance to the client's current difficulties.

When a memory has been selected, the therapist guides the client to access the memory by identifying its mental, emotional, and bodily components, and then assists the client to reprocess the memory. Reprocessing consists of a series of short segments (usually under a minute) in which the client is guided to simply observe a memory as his or her brain experiences it under these therapeutic conditions.

During each reprocessing segment, the therapist provides *dual attention* stimulation. Typically, this comes in the form of bilateral eye movements in which the therapist guides the client to move his or her eyes from side to side at a pace of about one second per pass. While this may sound a bit odd, many studies have shown that the eye-movement element of the therapy contributes to the accelerated reprocessing of the trauma memory.

Several neurobiological theories have been proposed to explain why eye movements are so effective. Perhaps the most readily understandable is that EMDR may replicate mental processes that take place during REM sleep, when eyes move rapidly from side to side. The REM phase of sleep is a small portion of total sleep, yet the time when the most active dreaming occurs. With the body at full rest, and conscious mental processes off-line, the brain is freed to do other work. As everyone knows, when people wake up after a good night's sleep, they often have a fresh approach to a nagging problem. Presumably, mental processes that occur during sleep have helped sort things out for them. Brain scans have mapped the robustly dynamic neurological processes that occur during REM sleep. Without conscious effort, sleep allows a person's mind to access existing knowledge and activate the imagination to come to a more effective and adaptive perspective on a problem. EMDR may stimulate some components of REM sleep to activate the internal processes that make dreams so effective. Experimentation has found that headphones producing side-to-side tones as well as side-to-side physical tapping can have similar effects to the eye movements.

During these reprocessing segments or "sets," the client is assisted by the therapist to digest the disturbing components of the memory bite by bite. Initially, the person is guided to picture the traumatic experience in his or her mind and is helped to tune in to all aspects of the memory, including its sensory, cognitive, emotional, and physiological components. During the eye-movement sets, clients are reminded to trust the brain to do its own healing and "just notice what happens." They may notice a range of memory fragments, including forgotten facts, emotions, and body responses. They also typically experience changes in memories, new associations, and new insights. After each set of eye movements, the therapist asks the client to briefly share what he or she is experiencing at that moment, though EMDR does not require a person to talk about the details of what happened. Typically, the therapist then directs the client back to the reprocessing. The therapist helps the client focus on appropriate material before starting each subsequent set. If the client becomes too distressed, the reprocessing is stopped while the therapist takes steps to address the concern and determine if and when the client would like to resume reprocessing. The client stays with a particular memory until the disturbance level associated with it is no longer present in his or her mind even when consciously remembering the experience.

EMDR facilitates the brain's innate capacity to process the trauma under safe conditions so that when a person remembers the event, the intense emotions that were connected to the memory fade. The person can think and talk about the event without being emotionally activated. The person can recall the event without reliving it. It becomes another part of that person's life history rather than a consuming and self-defining story. When the client reports no distress related to the targeted memory, the therapist helps the client identify the more positive perspective that has been attained, generally including a more positive view of oneself. For me, the effectiveness of EMDR has proven itself over and over again. While the process can seem a bit mystifying at first, the client often has an "aha" realization accompanied by the emergence of insight and positive changes in physical and emotional responses. Within a few sessions, most people can readily assess for themselves whether the treatment is working.

I trained in EMDR in 2002. I had heard many positive things about EMDR and was eager to learn new trauma-informed strategies to relieve the suffering of my clients. The training was conducted by Dr. Steven Silver, a psychologist and Marine combat veteran who is a pioneer in the use of EMDR with war veterans. He has worked with trauma survivors for more than forty years, including as director of the PTSD program at a VAMC in Coatesville, Pennsylvania. As he has also discussed in his book,[80] Silver talked about key elements that make war trauma so impactful. He emphasized the duration of exposure, the likelihood of multiple traumas, that war trauma is man-made, that the survivor is both perpetrator and victim, the conflicted role of the survivor, the mixed state of feeling both powerful and powerless, the witnessing of what happens to others leading to survivor guilt, and the societal impact of war.

Ben, the veteran I introduced at the start of this chapter, understood all of these elements of his war experience. He was eager to see if EMDR could help.

BEN'S SESSIONS

Ben had faced many disturbing combat experiences, but he told me that only two remained deeply etched in his mind. These two memories had crossed a line. He couldn't get past them, and they fueled his PTSD.

The older memory was of the first patient Ben saw die on an operating table in Iraq. The soldier was missing both legs and an arm from a bomb explosion, and the team worked desperately to manage the loss of blood. There was some hope of saving the man, and the procedure went on for more than an hour before he was pronounced dead. Ben wasn't the primary medical person in charge, nor was he responsible for the death in any way, but the experience lodged itself in his brain, and he couldn't shake it. The smell of blood was still distinct in his mind (smell is an especially raw and powerful sense, no doubt rooted in our evolutionary past). Ben remembered that experience vividly. He could picture the digital clock on the wall reading 14:20, the exact time they "called his death." He could remember the patient's blood pressure, heart rate, what the nurse was wearing, and what he was wearing. He couldn't put the experience out of his mind, and he couldn't comfort himself with thoughts like "you did the best you could." Rationally, he knew all that, but he couldn't sync up that information with his rock-solid frozen horror of watching this man die.

Ben reprocessed the memory with me using EMDR. We started with his attention focused on the memory of "the smell of iron in the wounded soldier's blood and the St. Michael's pendant he wore."

I asked him what lasting belief he had related to that memory. "I'm a failure," he said. I asked him what he would prefer to believe about himself. "That I am selfless, enduring, and capable." But to him at that moment, those words did not feel true. He said that as he recalled the memory, he felt anxiety, and he reported that the memory disturbed him at a level of eight on a zero-to-ten scale. When asked what he felt in his body, he said, "I can feel my heart rate increase, and my heart feels heavy."

At that point, I asked him to recall the smell of the blood and the pendant, and to notice any other feelings, as I led him through a series of back and forth eye movements. Each *set* of eye movements lasted about forty-five seconds. After each set, I asked him what he was noticing at that moment. His progression of observations between the sets of eye movements revealed some of his inner process as he worked though the memory. After the first set, he said, "I don't feel really in touch with anything right now." Then after the next set, he reported, "I'm just remembering a willingness to help and knowing I couldn't do anything." His level of disturbance dropped slightly to a six.

After the next set, he said, "I feel overwhelmed." I asked if he wanted to keep going, and he did. After another forty-five-second set of eye movements, he said, "I feel frustration that I can't get rid of it." This understandable feeling is a common early reaction. After the next set, he said, "I remember all the details of that day" and then rattled them off. After that, he said, "I feel numb." I asked him to back up to the last point he felt something. After the next set, "I have strong feelings in my hands," and then, "There are so many different things going on in my head it's too much to describe it to you. Flashing thoughts." Suddenly it was coming to him fast. I reassured him that these were his memory networks processing, and that I didn't need to know the details.

Next he said, "I remember the first image of when they came in with the patient. You never know what to expect. When you are in training and practice procedures on a dummy or your buddy, it's not very real. And then actually seeing somebody with no legs and this enormous welt. It just overtakes you." It was obvious Ben was deeply in touch with the memory and integrating it into his prior expectations. Another set of eye movements brought him to, "I'm going through the whole process of what happened from when he first arrived until it was over." True to the EMDR process, I did not stop to discuss Ben's experience; I just kept him moving through it.

After another set, he said, "I was thinking about the guy who was across from me that day. My friend Tim; he was my partner. . . ." And another set: "I was thinking about how Tim was my smoking buddy, and how after surgery we'd go have a cigarette and clean up the litter of all the blood and human matter. That was our time. We never really talked during that time but we would just be there doing our job. And I remember that day it was almost like our goodbye to the soldier we had lost." Ben could now realize that he was not alone, that his friend had been with him throughout the experience. Next set: "I was thinking about the same thing." By now, quiet tears were flowing from Ben and continued as he went on. After another set, he said, "I went back to thinking about Louie [this was the first time he had given a name to the patient], and how it's funny that I never met him or knew him personally, but he had more influence on me than anyone else in my life." Ben was spontaneously beginning to have positive thoughts about his patient replacing the despair.

After another set came, "I thought about the saying that 'war is old men talking and young men dying.' I think it's a way to deal with what had happened." Then, "It feels like it's getting numb," and after the next set came a spontaneous revelation, "I've thought about this a lot for five years. It's played over so much. I used to bawl my eyes out; just tearing up a bit is a victory for me."

Ben's tone was beginning to change. "I haven't thought about it hard core for about a year now but it's less disturbing now." His relief was evident. After another set he said, "It's a solid memory that will be with me for the rest of my life." Some more peaceful acceptance was building. Next, he commented, "As I look back on that now, it was the beginning of becoming what I was as a pathfinder medic. I learned a lot in that hospital. I worked under amazing doctors and nurses. I learned from them and made my skills a lot stronger than a lot of people." Ben's perspective was changing, and his spirits were lifting.

After the next set, he told me, "To me now, it's sad that Louie died and that he went out in probably the worst way possible. But I thank him a lot because he broke that barrier for me of knowing what I had to deal with." At that point I commented, "I can tell you honor him." Ben replied, "I'm getting chills up my spine as I see that I do honor him and I wish I could have thanked him." I said, "Well, just think about that and imagine thanking him." More tears followed as he continued to process the memory and the reparative opportunity to thank Louie.

After another set, he said, "I still have that feeling of ease and comfort." I asked, "Right now how disturbing is the memory, zero to ten?" He said, "Not disturbing, really. I know it is sad but I also see the other side. It doesn't weigh me down." I asked him if the positive phrase, "I'm selfless, enduring, and capable," felt more true to him now. He said it did.

So, this is how an EMDR reprocessing session can work. Over a series of reprocessing sets, Ben had progressed from haunting despair, to pure sadness, to realizing he was not alone, to relief from the pain. He was able to find a way to pay tribute to his patient and realize that he had grown wiser from that very same memory. Ben also finally grasped that the experience was truly over. Trauma had disoriented his perception of time. When the traumatic memory was triggered, part of his brain had understood what day and time it was, but the more emotional part of his brain did not. The old, emotionally charged memories had convinced his mind that the conditions of the past still existed. Even when he understood cognitively that the experience was in the past, he couldn't feel it. But now, as he reprocessed this traumatic memory, he began to separate from it. Its emotional intensity faded and no longer threatened him. He found a way of making peace with what had happened that day. In fact, he now realized that the event inspired him to be the best medic he could be.

At the next session, Ben reported that he was still in a good place related to the memory of Louie. So we moved to the second memory. This one was worse. Ben and three other soldiers were driving in a convoy in Afghanistan. Suddenly, there was a huge explosion, and the truck, which had driven over an IED, vaulted into the air and landed on its side. All the soldiers were injured and trapped in their positions, with Ben in the back of the vehicle. Ben's close friend was in the front, groaning. Ben could see that his friend was bleeding. As a medic, he believed that the friend was mortally injured, but he kept that thought to himself as he tried to comfort his friend. Although there were other trucks around, the protocol dictated that no one could come to the aid of these men until the area had been searched and cleared of other explosives. Past experience had taught the Army that the Taliban often planted two explosives in one area with the second one set to explode once rescuers had come to the aid of the first victims. Eventually, the area was cleared, and Ben and the other men were rescued from the truck. The friend was airlifted out of the area. Word came back to the unit the next day that he had died.

As part of the treatment process, I asked Ben to identify the specific components of the traumatic memory as he recalled them at that moment in my office. These components were a snapshot of the multiple parts of his traumatic memory that he still carried lodged intact in his brain. They intruded into his life, and any reminder of any one of these components could trigger and activate the whole package. They were as follows:

Sensory impressions: the sound of the explosion; the sudden darkness as the sand swirled around the vehicle; the intense heat that increased with time; the smells, the discomfort, and disorientation of being trapped in the vehicle; the pain in his leg from the accident.

Thoughts: "I can't move." "Another bomb may go off." "My friend is going to die."

Emotions: fear, helplessness.

Body sensations: "anxiousness in my chest."

Negative belief about himself: "I'm powerless."

Ben rated how disturbed he felt as he recalled these components in the present moment (not what he thinks he experienced at the time) as a nine on the ten-point scale. In my office, as he returned his attention to that moment in time, the memory components came alive as if he were back in that truck. The nature of an unresolved traumatic memory is that it appears frozen in time. The components lie like coiled springs. Once activated, the past becomes the present. But this time, he knew he was safe in the therapeutic process.

Again, we worked through Ben's memory with sets of eye movements alternating with expressions of what he was feeling and thinking. During each reprocessing segment, far more was occurring in his brain than he could put into words, or I could understand, for that matter. But this process kept him moving forward, as resolution takes place faster than the conscious mind can understand it. In fact, although intellectual insights come with this process, they are not the main goal. This distinguishes EMDR from models of therapy that focus primarily on conscious understanding. EMDR welcomes insight, but aims for more profound healing when a person is no longer emotionally and psychophysiologically troubled by something, whether he or she understands why or not.

Later, after Ben had faced and resolved this memory, it became an old memory of a tragic experience, not a memory that consumed him with the feelings of the moment. He could talk about it without fear, anxiety in his chest, or thinking of himself as powerless. The once-vivid sensations of heat and pain had faded. When I asked him how disturbing the memory was *now* on a zero-to-ten point scale, he said, "zero." He was still very sad about the loss of his friend, but the grief no longer immobilized him. He realized on a deep level that the experience was behind him, and there was nothing he could do about it. Up until that point, thinking of his buddy only brought pain. Now he could recall, talk about, and even laugh about some of the positive memories of his time with his friend.

INTEGRATION

Ben's healing demonstrates his own resilience. As veterans experience relief from their symptoms of PTSD or depression, they discover a capacity they had lost sight of. As traumatic memories are processed through EMDR, a more positive outlook develops. Not only are veterans able to move forward with their lives, but they view the past differently. They are better able to remember and take satisfaction from the positive aspects of their war experiences, including accomplishments, new skills, leadership opportunities, confidence, friendships, and benefits that come from veteran status.

The term *posttraumatic growth* has been used to acknowledge these gains. Phase three, integration, is about making sure these gains last. Many people leave therapy after they get significant relief from trauma resolution work, and you can't blame them. But more therapy sessions, even if less frequent, can help a person regain vitality, break bad habits, and design the next stage of life.

The emotional and cognitive changes from reprocessing often result in spontaneous behavioral and personal change. For example, a veteran who had withdrawn from social activities might now be willing to get together with friends. At times, Ben had held back from enjoying the company of his buddies who made it back because of the unresolved loss of his friend.

I do not want to suggest that everyone will get through war trauma memories as quickly as Ben did. And Ben, himself, continued to work on some other issues. Everyone is different, and a trained clinician will customize the treatment plan and expectations to the individual. But often traumatic memories turn out to be paper tigers. They are ferocious when they consume a person with fear. Yet, when finally faced under controlled conditions, these "tigers" can be dismantled into what they really are: *old* memories that are long gone and no longer relevant.

EMDR seems to kick-start the brain to undo the stuck nature of trauma memories. If a trauma memory is a block of ice, EMDR allows it to thaw. Presumably much of the healing or resolution of the memory takes place on an unconscious level as the brain changes a disturbing memory to an "adaptive resolution," including a more rational and balanced perspective on the memory. Often during the EMDR therapy, the client is able to access personal strengths and coping abilities and link them to the traumatic memory. This helps clients more fully understand that the experience is over, that they survived, and that they are fundamentally OK.

EMDR frees the client of the impact of PTSD. What remains from the trauma can be talked about with more detachment. What is of value from the past is retained to guide future experiences, but what is no longer needed or adaptive is discarded. The memories may still be unpleasant, but they are no longer intrusive. They are no longer experienced as if they were happening to the person in the present moment. This allows the person to relax and focus on what is important. It allows him or her to move forward in life rather than staying stuck in the past. With additional help, veterans can rediscover who they are now that they are freed from the trauma and build new life patterns.

Certainly, for many veterans there are very real challenges that remain, including the effects of physical wounds, including amputation, chronic physical pain, and TBI. However, the capacity to cope with these wounds is maximized when the psychological challenges are attended to.

BEN IS NOW headed to graduate school to become a physician's assistant. In his application, he shared his own experience and hard-earned wisdom, including this:

> *I served six years as an Army Medic, deploying twice to war to protect my fellow soldiers. As a medic, everyone depends on you for help and expects you to provide an instantaneous solution. I had to be smarter, to provide better care for my comrades, so I learned everything I could to help them survive. I needed to carry the biggest guy, so I became stronger. I had to cover my buddy when he was shot, so I became a better marksman. I lived my life to protect my companions, knowing that one day they could become my patients. Not only did I master skills in emergency treatment; I mastered skills to prevent injuries from occurring . . .*

What a difference from the Ben I first met who felt he hadn't done enough and was haunted by his war traumas!

Recently in a follow-up with Ben, I talked with him about his earlier suicidal feelings. He said he never was going to let them get the better of him but had dealt with them constantly. He told me frankly that while deployed he hated people who felt suicidal because it took time and energy to deal with them, and there was no time for that. His first supervisor in Iraq killed himself there—with fifteen counts of sexual harassment hanging over him, he went into a porta-potty and shot himself in the heart—and that put more burden on Ben. At age twenty-three, Ben suddenly had to step up and fill that position, which he kept for sixteen months.

In Afghanistan, Ben had helped send three guys home because of their suicidality. "A weakness and a plague," he considered it at that time because it depleted the unit. As the medic, though, he made it his business to monitor mental health issues in his unit and cared enough to protect those who were vulnerable. He still talks with these three men occasionally.

After being the go-to caretaker in the war zone, Ben suddenly was back in the States face-to-face with his own needs. "I didn't even care about my problems. I just threw them in the trash can and took care of everybody else. Then I realized that I wasn't a medic anymore, there was no one to take care of, and I didn't know what to do with myself."

He told me, "I battled suicide a lot because I didn't like what I did over there. I liked what I did for the people over there," but overall the war was a "mistake" and a "fucking sham . . . and I guarantee you that a lot of people who took their lives felt this way. They fought in another country and now they don't have anything to live for. So it sucks."

Still, Ben concluded, although "I lost so much, I just have to figure out how to keep moving on, and after the EMDR work on trauma, I kind of EMDRed the whole war. . . . I recommend to anybody that comes out of the military to do EMDR and talk about all the big moments. . . . I remember being so skeptical" about EMDR at first. "But now I'm a completely different person."

"I remember how I always said that the lack of control made me go crazy. Sounds and doors opening would send me wild. It doesn't do that anymore . . . I've been more relaxed and more soft-spoken lately. Probably for six or seven months now." Ben had a blowup with his brother a year earlier when he felt his brother didn't understand what he was going through and jumped on him about it. Ben reacted fiercely, and they didn't talk for months. But now they are close again.

As for suicidality, he says,

> I feel like the lowest point in getting your life back is thinking about suicide because it isolates you. But fighting it and over-coming it, the feeling that you overcame the greatest threat to yourself, it made me stronger . . . I don't know if I can explain the moment when it did go away or why it went away, but I know it has faded away. . . . I think the biggest part was just letting other people besides my inner circle see this and know what was going on. I know letting my brothers know helped a lot. Letting them see that I wasn't OK relieved the burden off my chest. In another sense I was afraid they'd treat me differently, that they'd put the gloves on and treat me real delicate. But they haven't.

And now, thinking back on the war, the trauma, the PTSD, and the suicidality, Ben says, "I like to purposely look back over my shoulder now and give it the finger and laugh."

chapter 10
MANY STORIES—KEEPING VETERANS VISIBLE

WITH THE WITHDRAWAL of U.S. combat forces from Afghanistan in late 2014, America now officially moves into a postwar era. Evidence from history, and from experiences like the Luceys', indicates that our society has a problem meeting the postwar needs of its service members, veterans, and their families. Many Americans do pause to acknowledge veterans and their service, but most of us are tired of these wars and want to move on. The psychologically and physically wounded veterans can become, sadly, an inconvenience for civilians preoccupied with challenges closer to home—work, family, and financial security. Many civilians do not really want to know the truth of war when it's over. Myths that vets are either superheroes or PTSD wrecks take hold because dealing with the complex reality takes more effort.

Dr. Mark Russell, an Iraq veteran and EMDR trainer with more than twenty-five years of military service, puts the recent wars in historical perspective. Once wars end, he writes, resources dry up, memories fade, and American society hits a national reset button, returning to the neglect of its veterans. Each year, Veterans Day brings forth lofty speeches, but the next morning a "collective amnesia descends again over the national landscape." Russell likens the current state of military psychological care to "preparing for surgical needs in war by supplying hacksaws and a biting stick."[81]

SEEING VETERANS

A good starting place for civilians is to take the time to actually *see* veterans—to remember that they exist and understand that they may operate a little differently (for better and for worse) as a result of being veterans. If you work with vets regularly, such as on college campuses, at social service agencies, or in treatment settings, I encourage you to learn about veterans' issues and concerns. Tune in to what veterans need. Read up on the subject and consider additional training, so you can respond skillfully.

Ten years after Jeff's death, his sister Debbie now works in protective services for the Department of Children and Families in Massachusetts. She has to remind her colleagues that finding out if someone is a veteran is a key part of a thorough family assessment. "So many factors in a family can be better understood if you realize that there is a veteran and if you have the right training," Debbie points out.

Debbie and her mother, Joyce, are now both volunteers for the Tragedy Assistance Program for Survivors (TAPS) and serve as mentors to other families who are survivors of military-related suicides. Kevin, Joyce, and Debbie serve as field advocates for the American Foundation for the Prevention of Suicide, and they continue to be invited to speaking engagements.

Kevin Lucey, a former probation officer, has supported and helped promote the new veterans' courts in Massachusetts, where judges who are sensitive to veterans' issues hold weekly sessions to address the criminal and substance abuse problems of veterans. The idea started in 2008 in Buffalo, New York, and has spread to at least 130 other courts nationally. Vets return to the court weekly for a year or two, and judges help them stay on track ("right the ship" as one judge put it) in terms of treatment and employment, through the support of a veteran-specific setting where other vets are present and where the space can be made welcoming for vets (for example, by lining one courtroom with military flags).[82] It seems like a small matter, but creating familiarity and a sense of community for veterans makes a big difference in how services and resources are received.

Easy-to-access resources are now developing, such as vets4warriors.com, stopsoldiersuicide.org, Team Red, White and Blue, and many, many more, to help veterans and their families connect or to find help in a crisis.

The Corporal Jeffrey M. Lucey Chapter of Veterans for Peace in Hyannis, Massachusetts, was the first VFP chapter to name itself after a veteran who committed suicide. The members further dedicated themselves to the cause of suicide prevention and remain in close touch with the Luceys.

The Luceys, other military families, some parts of the government, and other program providers have done a lot to address the needs of veterans. But this needs to become a priority in civilian society as a whole. Some civilians need to sort out their own issues about military and combat service, including values and opinions related to our most recent wars. We need to separate the war from the warrior, the military from militarism. We need to be prepared to hear difficult things and not flinch. When the veteran says, "You probably can't help me," civilians need to be able to respond honestly and helpfully in order to close the gap of understanding.[83]

War veterans and civilians alike hold a longstanding belief that civilians can never understand the experience of battle. That was Jeff's mantra. This clearly has truth to it, but nonveterans of war should not be easily deterred by this myth as they seek to listen and learn. As a therapist, I look at extreme versions of this attitude as a *blocking belief*, that is, one more obstacle that interferes with a veteran's accepting help. Other blocking beliefs include, "If I tell someone they'll be overwhelmed, or they'll judge me, or I'll lose respect." In Jeff's case, he believed that if he told people what bothered him at his debriefing at Camp Pendleton, he'd be detained from going home. Later, he feared that if he was admitted to the VA, it would ruin his career. In the case of war-related PTSD, the tendency to isolate from others can exacerbate the belief that no one understands, leading to resignation.

The military system is masterful at creating an esprit de corps that bonds units together. How else could service personnel do such difficult things and be so loyal to their buddies? Friendship with war buddies is one the most lasting experiences a war veteran can hold onto. The special bond among war veterans is a powerful asset, but it can become a liability if it walls off veterans from trusting civilians. The downside of that bonding process is an us-against-them mentality that often pits military branches against each other and even divides members of a unit who had different experiences. And that mindset can be transferred to people back home who supposedly can never understand. That attitude contributes to veterans' tendency toward isolation and the resentment that comes with it. For the risks and sacrifices our troops have made, civilians have a responsibility to try to bridge that gap.

Fortunately, I have never personally been through many of the traumatic experiences that my clients come to address in therapy, such as childhood deprivation, physical or sexual abuse, racial discrimination, battling cancer, or surviving life-threatening circumstances. Yet I have worked to perfect my craft of helping people face their issues with empathy and structured guidance. All civilians have good questions and special qualities they can bring to conversations with veterans to help them share their stories and feel more at home in the civilian world.

THE VETERANS EDUCATION PROJECT

The Veterans Education Project (VEP), which I've mentioned earlier, is an example of a local, volunteer group working to bridge that divide between veterans and civilians. Its leaders, Rob Wilson and Susan Leary, convey great respect for the experiences of veterans, perhaps the core starting place in a conversation with any veteran. Like me, they never served in the military yet felt compelled to understand and make accessible the stories of veterans.

In its own grassroots way, the VEP, which began in 1982, was part of a larger national trend in the aftermath of the Vietnam War, one that included the Vietnam Memorial (The Wall) and the film *Platoon*, for example. The VEP and others sought to illuminate the legacy of the war by featuring veterans who told the truth about what they had experienced. They sought to de-glorify war by exposing the harsh realities and consequences of war and debunking the myths put forth by exploitative films such as *Rambo*. VEP speakers routinely share their mental-health, medical, and spiritual journeys toward recovery from traumas as well.

Not long ago, I participated in a memorable VEP presentation in Brattleboro, Vermont, attended by about fifty participants in a graduate mental-health program. The panel included myself, Ben (who you read about in chapter 9), his wife Kate, and Joe, a Vietnam veteran. I spoke about my awakening to veterans' needs through Jeff Lucey and then offered an overview on the war zone/home zone transition, clinical indicators of PTSD, risk factors and warning signs for suicide, and treatment options. Ben then told his own story. He had volunteered to speak for the VEP when he heard about their work. The VEP understands that sharing a story can also lead to a re-experiencing of a traumatic event, so safeguards are built in to prepare and debrief the presenters. Likewise, I was somewhat concerned that Ben might feel too exposed once he was standing in front of a large group, so we prepared as best we could.

Ben didn't talk about his formerly traumatic memories but rather told stories of his duties as a medic and described tough decisions he was forced to make under battle conditions. I was impressed with his poise, though he was clearly emotional as he spoke, and I took satisfaction in knowing that he could never have shared these details had he not done the therapeutic work. After Ben, Kate spoke. Kate was able to be frank about the strain on her during his deployments and on their relationship as Ben tried to readjust in this country. She spoke of moments like when Ben flew into a rage when he couldn't get the air conditioner into the window. She wasn't afraid of him, but she felt helpless as he just kept slamming it around. Now, Ben takes a walk if he's upset.

Then Joe spoke. He was also a medic in the army, but a generation earlier in Vietnam. He was awarded the Bronze Star, with a "V" for valor, the Purple Heart, the Army Commendation Medal, and a Combat Medic's Badge for more than a year of war-zone service ending in 1969. He spoke with vivid details about being ambushed and watching as a battalion-sized unit of the North Vietnamese Army comprising hundreds of soldiers walked by as he and three others hid. He spoke of a friend who fell into a raging river and that commanders did not stop the mission to recover his body. "I had enough hate for the stupid decisions that were made all of the time by superiors to make me fly into a rage at that point. We were all just pawns to the brigade-level officers. Feelings were never considered when the mission was jeopardized."

Joe also talked about his own personal jungle back home as he entered a thirty-year downward spiral, including alcohol and drug abuse, despite holding a job in the postal service before on-the-job behavior led to a suspension. That crash sparked his willingness to accept treatment from the Leeds VAMC, where he learned he had PTSD and began his personal recovery. He is grateful for their help, and his public speaking service is to lessen the chance that other veterans will take as long as he did to return to health.

The VEP format invites audiences to ask questions of the panelists, but this part of the program invariably starts with expressions of gratitude to the veterans who have spoken. The questions that afternoon were quite specific, and I watched as Ben and the others went from speaking to a roomful of unknown people to talking with each questioner, trying best to answer the inquiry in a useful way. When the event was over, Joe and Ben spoke and showed great interest in each other's stories from Vietnam and from Afghanistan.

The VEP and its presentations do not take political positions on war, but having been part of many of these presentations, I can say that no one goes away taking war lightly.

Theater events and film showings offer other opportunities for therapeutic storytelling. On September 11, 2011, I cosponsored a two-part event that began with a day-long training session on treating combat veterans and ended with a night at the theater. At the training, Ted Olejnik and two of his colleagues from the VA spoke to more than seventy people on topics of PTSD, suicidality, TBI, sleep disorders, and EMDR treatment. A fourth trainer for the Springfield Vet Center brought a video clip of a Humvee being flipped in Iraq by an

IED. Although we were reassured that no one was killed in the actual incident, the audience gasped as we watched this very small glimpse of war reality.

At the end of the professional workshop, we attended a local play, *Ambush on T Street*, which was an original theatrical performance created and performed by a Vietnam veteran/farmer/poet, a musician, and a writer/actor. Cosponsored by the VEP and other local groups, it was an autobiographical exploration of trauma and healing. In the play, the paths of these three men collide. One is a homeless vet struggling to piece together his bombed-out life. The second is a street musician obsessed with his failed career and history as a psychiatric patient, and the third is a burned-out counselor with an office on the same street. The sharing of their personal stories brings them out of their isolation and starts the process of healing old wounds. In one remarkable moment in the play, the veteran is talking to a priest who is trying to console him about his war trauma, in which he killed an eighteen-year-old boy who he thought to be a threat but who turned out to be harmless. The veteran utters in agony, "Maybe, Father, but standing over the body of a dying boy that you have shot, there is no separation between the killer and the one who is killed. Both are dying."

ONE HUNDRED FACES OF WAR EXPERIENCE

A more visual type of storytelling infuses the remarkable project of Matthew Mitchell, an artist here in Amherst, that acknowledges participants from America's recent wars. He calls it "100 Faces of War Experience."

Mitchell has been painting portraits of Americans who went into the recent wars, including service members, contractors, a journalist, and an activist. Each is accompanied by a statement in his or her own words. Representing a wide range of geography, race, age, gender, and outcomes (some are dead, some wounded, some healthy), the portraits connect civilians viscerally with the Americans who went to Iraq and Afghanistan. Mitchell's portrait of an Army sergeant disfigured in an IED explosion has hung in the National Portrait Gallery in Washington, DC.

Mitchell's first portrait was of Jeff Lucey, painted after his death. They had never met. Sitting down with Kevin and Joyce Lucey, Mitchell felt he was "entering a different world" since he didn't know anyone in the military or feel that the wars had affected his life directly. Connecting the military and civilian worlds is a central goal of Mitchell's project. He is seeing, listening to, and trying to understand veterans. But it doesn't come easily.

As part of his artistic process, Mitchell has visited active duty troops and veterans in their homes, at military bases, and in military and VA hospitals across the county. Though his portraits are central in his exhibitions, Mitchell conducted extensive interviews and listened to the veterans' stories of their military experiences before capturing them on canvas. Each portrait is exhibited along with a synopsis or other reflections written by the subjects. In cases where a veteran was killed or took his own life, Mitchell painted the portrait from photographs, and family members constructed the accompanying text. He recently completed all one hundred portraits, and they can be viewed at 100facesofwarexperience.org or at his traveling exhibitions.

I met Matt one evening for dinner at an outdoor café, along with a friend and colleague of mine named Jim Helling. Jim is a psychotherapist with an expertise in trauma and, in a previous career, was an embedded photojournalist during the 1991 Gulf War. Jeff was Matt's first and most challenging portrait, and Matt had consulted with Jim when he found himself overwhelmed and artistically blocked as he tried to understand and capture Jeff's essence.

Matt told me the project had started when he read about a "Welcome Home Vet" dinner—yet another local project in our area trying to connect civilians with veterans early in the Iraq War. It was 2005, and Matt "really wanted to do something that brings the meaning of the war home to America and reaches across all the different political viewpoints, and try to find the common ground that human life matters to everyone." But Matt realized that his "lack of knowledge and connection to the war was incredible. I had feelings about it but no real link to anything. . . . None of my parents, siblings or grandparents on either side served." He read about an artist, Steven

Mumford, who had gone to Iraq to do drawings and paintings of the war, saying he "didn't want to do art based on television." Matt realized that everything he knew about Iraq came from television. "All of a sudden there it was. The human portrait is something I already had an interest in."

He had read about Jeff in the newspaper and contacted the Luceys about doing a portrait of Jeff, about ten months after Jeff's death. "They were surprisingly receptive." Matt's hometown had seen a number of suicides, and he was well aware of the "dark stain on the person and the family." When he met the Luceys, "I was surprised but impressed that they were absolutely convinced that being open was their way to do things." At the time, nobody was connecting suicide with the war. "No one was thinking that way," Matt recalled.

At that point, Matt had only a slight idea of doing more than just the one portrait. But as Jim pointed out, the project evolved into something "really quite far-reaching. Each portrait is part of a larger process of making a huge collection of portraits. This collection creates a much larger image. And trying to grasp that image is really an experience. It's extremely radical and extremely sophisticated. So if you focus too narrowly on Jeff and his portrait you miss his place in the whole of this." Matt settled on the idea of a large number, a hundred portraits, "to represent the idea that this is a massive thing. In my gallery exhibitions, people are surrounded by faces. Just the sheer quantity of images and the amount of labor that people know went into these portraits reflects the magnitude of the issue." The project took nearly a decade to complete.

At first, Matt focused on the paintings themselves, but over time the stories became a huge part of it. The stories were what helped him understand the person he was painting. Kevin advised him that listening was going to be a big part of his project. "The extraordinary thing is I didn't realize until years later how much these people were trusting me as an artist. Kevin and I talked for hours and then he showed me photos. There were times when I had no idea what to say. I felt like an infant." To paint the portrait right, he had to see the world, and the war, through the eyes of his subjects. It was painful. At times he cried.

Painting Jeff's portrait meant seeing the world through the eyes of someone so devoid of hope that he had killed himself. "In a lot of ways," Matt told me, "the portrait doesn't really look like Jeff, but I was piecing together photographs from different times of his life.... I had to take different pictures from these different times and try to figure out what his future would be like. In his face, I tried to extrapolate from Joyce and Kevin's faces as well.... Every little teeny movement in a person's face is incredibly significant. I was pulling on the photos that I saw and the stories that I heard."

I told Matt that when I first saw Jeff's portrait, what struck me was that it was grittier than photographs I had seen, and he looked a bit older than when he died. The image was raw, unpolished. I was captivated as I gazed at it, though I cringed a bit at the emotional impact. He looked strong and serious, conveying a sobriety that seemed to reflect all that he'd been through. The portrait seemed to blend the part of Jeff that was OK with the part of him that was not. Matt replied, "You seeing that is the most I could hope for."

Matt Mitchell's portrait of Jeff, 2005.

Jeff's portrait took several months to paint. Matt had to pull away from it at times and work on other portraits. "I realized something was blocking me with Jeff's picture. When I'd talk to people about the project I'd almost end up in tears." Finally, a friend suggested consulting a trauma specialist, and Matt said, "Well, of course!" That's when he brought in Jim.

Why did Matt spend ten years painting one hundred portraits of people he didn't know? Probably for the same reason that all artists with an inner inspiration can work tirelessly to express themselves through their chosen medium. But the other extraordinary thing that Matt did, that we can all learn from, was to take a flying leap across the divide between unknowing civilians and isolated veterans. Coming from a starting point of no military background, no knowledge of the wars other than the superficial TV version, with no connections, no money or sponsors, he set out to see, listen to, and understand not one person but a hundred.

Matt did not accept that "you could never understand." He tried to understand. It was very hard and very slow. But he kept at it.

So here is America's challenge: To recognize that the end of the war is not the end of the battle. That peace is only a beginning. That politicians' talk about a sacred obligation to veterans needs to be accompanied by real and sustained resources to help veterans heal, not only in the VA itself but across all our communities, not only with money and jobs but with attitude and effort by those who didn't serve. Military PTSD is not just a veterans' problem or our military families' problem or the VA's problem. It is a national problem, indeed a wound to the nation itself, and only together can we heal it.

* * * * *

For more, visit this book's website at WoundsWithin.com

HELP IS AVAILABLE

THIS BOOK DISCUSSES difficult and sometimes painful subjects. Help is available through these resources:

Military/VA crisis hotline (Veterans and active-duty service members), **1-800-273-8255** (and **press 1)**, chat online at www. VeteransCrisisLine.net, or text to **838255**. In Europe, call **00800 1273 8255** or **DSN 118***. In Korea, call **0808 555 118** or **DSN 118**.

Tragedy Assistance Program for Survivors (TAPS), 1-800-959-TAPS (1-800-959-8277), or online at www.taps.org.

To find a private therapist trained in EMDR (Eye Movement Desensitization and Reprocessing), see the EMDR International Association, www.emdria.org.

This book is not intended as psychotherapy advice, which should be sought from a licensed therapist.

ACKNOWLEDGMENTS

THIS BOOK IS written with special recognition of Jeff Lucey, whose painful and consuming ordeal ultimately brought so much to light. It is my deep hope that this book assists war veterans in having the wisdom and courage to identify and heal from the wounds within.

The book is written with the full authorization and cooperation of the Luceys, who shared all the information available to them, including private notes and writings. Much of the story is based on their accounts of events. They put no limits on what I wrote in the book. Upon request, they read the drafts of the manuscript and offered many helpful corrections to ensure accuracy. I am extremely grateful for their help and for their ongoing contributions to critical issues. To Kevin, Joyce, Debbie, and Kelly: Your bravery is an inspiration to me.

The book has also benefited greatly from the many therapists who taught me about trauma, PTSD, and EMDR treatment, in particular those whose knowledge included extensive experience with veterans, including Steve Silver, Susan Rogers, E. C. Hurley, and Ted Olejnik. For sharing their stories with me and letting me write about them, I thank Pablo Chaverri, Jaime Perez, Ted Olejnik, Michelle Williams, Rob Wilson, Joe Ames, Matt Mitchell, and of course my therapy clients who I have left anonymous.

Several people read and commented on previous drafts of this book, including Steve Silver, Jim Helling, Rob Wilson, Sue Butkus, George Abbott, Farnsworth Lobenstine, Tom Kovar, Stuart Bicknell, Rich McNally, Eric Hamburg, and Colleen Turner.

My wife Ann della Bitta and my daughter Geneva della Bitta-Nickerson read multiple drafts and made many useful editorial suggestions. My daughter Vanessa della Bitta-Nickerson helped draft Chapter 5 and develop the narrative tone of the book.

I especially want to thank my coauthor Joshua Goldstein who helped shepherd this book from idea stage to publication. His broad knowledge of war and society is interwoven throughout the book. Joshua's encouragement, along with his writing and editing talents, has been crucial in bringing my story to the printed page.

Our literary agent Fredrica S. Friedman has been at our side through the ups and downs of bringing this book to print and contributed many ideas as it took form. Thanks, Fredi!

Finally, both coauthors would like to thank all those who have served in uniform, their loved ones, and their clinicians. May they enjoy the blessings of peace.

NOTES

1   TBI data from Department of Defense, accessed Jan. 2, 2014 at dvbic.dcoe.mil/dod-worldwide-numbers-tbi. PTSD data: Our reference to 300,000 cases is conservative. Institute of Medicine (IOM), *Treatment for Posttraumatic Stress Disorder in Military and Veteran Populations: Initial Assessment* (Washington, DC: The National Academies Press, 2012), p.1, estimates that 13 to 20 percent of the 2.6 million who deployed (i.e., 338,000 to 520,000) "have or may develop PTSD." For PTSD among veterans using VA care, see Bagalman, Erin. *Mental Disorders among OEF/OIF Veterans Using VA Health Care: Facts and Figures.* Congressional Research Service, Feb. 4, 2013. For PTSD within active duty while deployed, see Fischer, Hannah. *A Guide to U.S. Military Casualty Statistics: Operation New Dawn, Operation Iraqi Freedom, and Operation Enduring Freedom.* Congressional Research Service, Feb. 19, 2014. See also McNally, Richard J. Psychiatric Casualties of War. *Science* 313, 2006: 923-24; Richardson, Lisa K., B. Christopher Frueh, and Ronald Acierno. Prevalence Estimates of Combat-Related PTSD: A Critical Review. *Australian and New Zealand Journal of Psychiatry* 4 (1), Jan. 2010: 4-19.

2   VA data accessed April 23, 2014 at www.vba.va.gov/reports/aspiremap.asp. The backlog peaked in 2013 at more than 600,000, and the extent of progress since then is disputed. See Maffucci, Jacqueline, *The Battle to End the VA Backlog.* Iraq and Afghanistan Veterans of America, Feb. 2014.

3   Goodwin, Jim. The Etiology of Combat-Related Post-Traumatic Stress Disorders. In Tom Williams, ed. *Post-Traumatic Stress Disorders: Handbook for Clinicians*. Cincinnati: Disabled American Veterans, 1987: 1-18.

4   Thompson, Mark and Nancy Gibbs. More U.S. Soldiers Have Killed Themselves than Have Died in the Afghan War. Why Can't the Army Win the War on Suicide? *Time*, July 23, 2012. Williams, Timothy. Suicides Outpacing War Deaths for Troops. *The New York Times*, June 8, 2012. Childress, Sarah. Why Soldiers Keep Losing to Suicide. PBS *Frontline*, Dec. 20, 2012. Zoroya, Gregg. Suicides of Young Vets Top Those of Active-Duty Troops. *USA Today*, Jan. 10, 2014. Zoroya, Gregg. War-years military suicide rate higher than believed. *USA Today*, Apr. 25, 2014.

5   Solomon, Jon. Military Suicide by Police in Dothan. Blog.al.com [Alabama], Nov. 1, 2012.

6   Swofford, Anthony. We Pretend the Vets Don't Even Exist. *Newsweek*, May 28, 2012.

7   Korb, Lawrence J. The Enemy Within. *Foreign Policy*, Oct. 9, 2012.

8   Kristof, Nicholas D. A Veteran's Death, the Nation's Shame. *The New York Times*, Apr. 14, 2012. Kristof, Nicholas D. War Wounds. *The New York Times*, Aug. 10, 2012.

9   Cox, Erin. Army Pauses Operations for Mandatory Suicide Prevention Training. *The Baltimore Sun*, Sept. 26, 2012. Lyle, Amaani. Panetta Discusses Efforts to Tackle Suicide. U.S. Department of Defense. American Forces Press Service, Sept. 24, 2012.

10 Dean, Eric T., Jr. *Shook over Hell: Post-Traumatic Stress, Vietnam, and the Civil War*. Cambridge, MA: Harvard University Press, 1999.

11 Leed, Eric J. *No Man's Land: Combat and Identity in World War I*. Cambridge, UK: Cambridge University Press, 1979: 174-75.

12 Ambrose, Stephen E. *Citizen Soldiers: The U.S. Army from the Normandy Beaches to the Bulge to the Surrender of Germany, June 7, 1944–May 7, 1945*. New York: Simon & Schuster, 1997: 329-30.

13 Dao, James. Vietnam Veterans, Discharged under Cloud, File Suit Saying Trauma Was Cause. *The New York Times*, Dec. 3, 2012: A12.

14 Greene, Bob. *Homecoming: When the Soldiers Returned from Vietnam.* New York: G. P. Putnam's Sons, 1989.

15 Gorlick, Adam. Marine Returns from Iraq to Emotional Ruin, Suicide. Associated Press, Oct. 16, 2004.

16 Hero Project TV on Daily Beast TV, Oct. 26, 2012.

17 Buchanan, Christopher. A Reporter's Journey. PBS *Frontline*, March 1, 2005 [segment of "The Soldier's Heart."] See www.pbs.org/wgbh/pages/frontline/shows/heart/lucey/.

18 Ibid.

19 Ibid.

20 Ibid.

21 Gorlick, 2004. See note 15.

22 Davis, Brian. Exclusive! Interview with Shinedown Vocalist Brent Smith. May 17, 2004. http://www.knac.com/article.asp?ArticleID=3009.

23 Wilson, John P., Matthew J. Friedman, and Jacob D. Lindy. *Treating Psychological Trauma and PTSD.* New York: Guilford, 2004.

24 U.S. Marine Corps. Investigation of the Death of Lance Corporal Jeffrey M. Lucey and the Allegations of War Crimes Made by Lance Corporal Lucey to His Father. August 16, 2004.

25 Buchanan, 2005. See note 17.

26 Ibid.

27 Shays, Jonathan. *Achilles in Vietnam: Combat Trauma and the Undoing of Character.* New York: Simon & Schuster, 1995. Maguen, Shira and Brett Litz. Moral Injury in Veterans of War. *PTSD Research Quarterly* 23 (1), 2012: 1-3. Meehan, Shannon P. Distant Wars, Constant Ghosts. *The New York Times*, Feb. 22, 2010.

28 AFSC, Eyes Wide Open exhibit, Boston, State House, Oct. 2005.

29 Rieckhoff, Paul. *Chasing Ghosts: Failures and Facades in Iraq: A Soldier's Perspective.* New York: Penguin, 2006.

30 Herbert, Bob. Death of a Marine. *New York Times*, March 19, 2007.

31 Silver, Steven M. and Rogers, Susan. *Light in the Heart of Darkness: EMDR and the Treatment of War and Terrorism Survivors.* New York: W.W. Norton, 2002.

32 Anyone needing help or information can call TAPS' toll-free line at 1-800-959-TAPS (8277).

33 Ashlock, Alex. Families Observe Suicide Prevention Day. National Public Radio, "Here and Now," Sept. 10, 2013.

34 Dreazen, Yochi. *The Invisible Front: Love and Loss in an Era of Endless War*. New York: Crown, 2014.

35 Dao, James. Families of Military Suicides Seek White House Condolences. *The New York Times*, Nov. 25, 2009.

36 Department of Veterans Affairs, Office of Inspector General. Healthcare Inspection—Review of Quality of Care Involving a Patient Suicide. John D. Daigh, Jr. M.D., Assistant Inspector General for Healthcare Inspections. Report No. 05-02562-124. Apr. 7, 2006.

37 See also Anestis, Michael D. *et al.* Understanding Suicidal Behavior in the Military: An Evaluation of Joiner's Interpersonal-Psychological Theory of Suicidal Behavior in Two Case Studies of Active Duty Post-Deployers. *Journal of Mental Health Counseling* 31 (1), 2009: 60-75.

38 Keteyian, Armen. VA Struggles with Vets' Mental Health. CBS News, Nov. 14, 2007.

39 Gura, David. Army Vice Chief Peter Chiarelli Addresses Soldier Suicides, Drug Abuse. National Public Radio, "All Things Considered," July 29, 2010.

40 See also Black, Sandra A. *et al.* Prevalence and Risk Factors Associated with Suicides of Army Soldiers 2001-2009. *Military Psychology* 23, 2011: 433-51. Ramchand, Rajeev *et al. The War Within: Preventing Suicide in the U.S. Military*. Santa Monica, CA: RAND [Prepared for the Office of the Secretary of Defense], 2011. Harrell, Margaret C. and Nancy Berglass. *Losing the Battle: The Challenge of Military Suicide*. Center for a New American Security, Policy Brief, October 2011. Carey, Benedict. Suicidal Tendencies Are Evident before Deployment, Study Finds. *The New York Times*, Mar. 4, 2014: A10.

41 Jaffe, Greg. Army's Vice Chief of Staff, Gen. Peter W. Chiarelli, Gives Closing Words of Advocacy. *Washington Post*, Jan. 28, 2012.

42 Call **1-800-273-8255** and **press 1**, chat online at www.VeteransCrisisLine.net, or text to **838255**.

43 Finkel, David. *Thank You for Your Service*. New York: Sarah Crichton, 2013: 72-80, 128-30, 198-200.

44 Ibid.: 207-8.

45 Thompson and Gibbs, 2012. See note 4.

46 VA/DoD Clinical Practice Guidelines: Management of Post-Traumatic Stress Disorder and Acute Stress Reaction. 2010. See www.healthquality.va.gov/guidelines/MH/ptsd/.

47 American Psychiatric Association. *Diagnostic and Statistical Manual of Mental Disorders*, Fifth Edition [DSM-5]. Arlington, VA: American Psychiatric Association, 2013.

48 Boon, Suzette, Kathy Steele, and Onno van der Hart. *Coping with Trauma Related Dissociation: Skills Training for Patients and Therapists*. New York: W.W. Norton, 2011.

49 American Psychiatric Association, DSM-5, 2013. See note 47.

50 Herman, Judith Lewis. *Trauma and Recovery*. New York: Basic Books, 1992: 1-3.

51 MacLean, Paul D. *The Triune Brain in Evolution: Role in Paleocerebral Functions*. New York: Plenum Press, 1990.

52 Bremner, J. Douglas. *Does Stress Damage the Brain? Understanding Trauma-related Disorders from a Mind–Body Perspective*. New York: Norton, 2005.

53 Goldstein, Joshua S. *War and Gender: How Gender Shapes the War System and Vice Versa*. Cambridge University Press, 2001: 254.

54 Grossman, Dave. *On Killing: The Psychological Cost of Learning to Kill in War and Society*. Boston: Little Brown, 1995.

55 Goodwin, 1987. See note 3.

56 Herman, 1992. See note 50.

57 See also Wilson, Suzanne. Troubled Mind. *Daily Hampshire Gazette*, Nov. 19, 2012: 1.

58 Risen, James. Military Has Not Solved Problem of Sexual Assault, Women Say. *The New York Times*, Nov. 2, 2012: A15. Brown, Patricia Leigh. For Female Veterans, a Struggle to Find a Home. *The New York Times*, Feb. 28, 2013: A.

59 The war zone and home zone concept was developed by the U.S. Army's "Battlemind" program, now known as Resilience Training.

60 U.S. Army. "PDHRA Battlemind Training: Continuing the Transition Home." fhp.osd.mil/pdhrainfo/media/battlemind_brochure.pdf.

61 Morrison, Marjorie. Are Our Vets Getting a Bum Rap? *Huffington Post*, Dec. 8, 2012.

62 The Beck Depression Inventory (BDI, BDI-1A, BDI-II), created by Dr. Aaron T. Beck, is a twenty-one-question, multiple-choice self-report inventory.

63 Fussell, Paul. *The Great War and Modern Memory*. Oxford University Press, 1975: 108.

64 Van der Kolk, Bessel A. The Body Keeps the Score: Memory and the Evolving Psychobiology of Posttraumatic Stress. *Harvard Review of Psychiatry*, Jan./Feb. 1994: 253-65.

65 Sherman, Michelle D. *et al.* Domestic Violence in Veterans with Posttraumatic Stress Disorder Who Seek Couples Therapy. *Journal of Marital and Family Therapy* 32 (4), 2006: 479–90. Novaco, Raymond W. and Claude M. Chemtob. Anger and combat-related posttraumatic stress disorder. *Journal of Traumatic Stress* 15, 2002: 123-32. Riggs, David S. Posttraumatic stress disorder and the perpetration of domestic violence. *PTSD Clinical Quarterly* 7 (2), 1997: 22-25.

66 Blake, Molly. Married to the Marines. *The New York Times* "At War" blog, May 21, 2013.

67 Aranda, Maj. Mary Catherine *et al.* Psychosocial Screening in Children with Wartime-deployed Parents. *Military Medicine* 176 (4), 2011: 402-7. Jensen, Peter S., David Martin, and Henry Watanabe. Children's Response to Parental Separation during Operation Desert Storm. *Journal of the American Academy of Child and Adolescent Psychiatry* 35 (4), 1996: 433-41.

68 Fantz, Ashley. *The Uncounted*: CNN report. March 2014. See www.cnn.com/interactive/2014/03/us/uncounted-suicides/.

69 Cosgrove, Lisa, Mary E. Brady, and Patricia Peck. PTSD and the Family: Secondary Traumatization. In Dennis K. Rhoads, Michael R. Leavack, and James C. Hudson, eds. *The Legacy of the Vietnam Veterans and their Families: Survivors of War, Catalysts for Change*. Washington, DC: Government Printing Office, 1995: 38-49.

70 Harkness, Laurie L. The effect of combat-related PTSD on children. *National Center for PTSD Clinical Newsletter* 2 (1991): 12-13.

71 Ancharoff, Michelle R., James F. Munroe, and Lisa Fisher. The Legacy of Combat Trauma: Clinical Implications of Intergenerational Transmission. In Yael Danieli, ed. *International Handbook of Multigenerational Legacies of Trauma.* New York: Plenum, 1998: 257-76.

72 Boss, Pauline. *Ambiguous Loss: Learning to Live with Unresolved Grief.* Cambridge, MA: Harvard University Press, 2000.

73 Van Winkle, Clint. *Soft Spots: A Marine's Memoir of Combat and Post-Traumatic Stress Disorder.* New York: St. Martin's, 2009: 28-31.

74 Cloitre, Marylene *et al.* Therapeutic Alliance, Negative Mood Regulation, and Treatment Outcome in Child Abuse-related Posttraumatic Stress Disorder. *Journal of Consulting and Clinical Psychology* 72, 2004: 411–16.

75 VA/DoD, 2010. See note 46.

76 Shapiro, Francine. *Eye Movement Desensitization and Reprocessing: Basic Principles, Protocols and Procedures*, 2nd ed. New York: Guilford, 2001.

77 More information at EMDR Institute, emdr.com, and EMDR International Association, emdria.org.

78 VA/DoD, 2010. See note 46.

79 Russell, Mark C. *et al.* Responding to an Identified Need: A Joint Department of Defense/Department of Veterans Affairs Training Program in Eye Movement Desensitization and Reprocessing (EMDR) for Clinicians Providing Trauma Services. *International Journal of Stress Management* 14, 2007: 61-71.

80 Silver and Rogers, 2002. See note 31.

81 Russell, Mark C. Best Way to Honor America's Veterans: End the Cycle of Mental Health Neglect, Stigma, and Crisis. *Huffington Post*, Nov. 11, 2012.

82 Lavoie, Denise. Mass Veterans Look to Treatment Court for Help. *Boston Globe*, Dec. 26, 2013.

83 Klay, Phil. After War, a Failure of the Imagination. *The New York Times*, Feb. 8, 2014. Bacevich, Andrew J. *Breach of Trust: How Americans Failed Their Soldiers and Their Country.* New York: Metropolitan, 2013.

INDEX

Note: Page numbers in italics indicate photographs.